the
elephant
in the
playroom

Ordinary Parents Write Intimately and Honestly
About Raising Kids with Special Needs

Denise Brodey

A PLUME BOOK

PLUME
Published by the Penguin Group
Penguin Group (USA) Inc., 375 Hudson Street, New York, New York 10014, U.S.A. •
Penguin Group (Canada), 90 Eglinton Avenue East, Suite 700, Toronto, Ontario,
Canada M4P 2Y3 (a division of Pearson Penguin Canada Inc.) • Penguin Books Ltd.,
80 Strand, London WC2R 0RL, England • Penguin Ireland, 25 St. Stephen's Green,
Dublin 2, Ireland (a division of Penguin Books Ltd.) • Penguin Group (Australia),
250 Camberwell Road, Camberwell, Victoria 3124, Australia (a division of Pearson
Australia Group Pty. Ltd.) • Penguin Books India Pvt. Ltd., 11 Community Centre,
Panchsheel Park, New Delhi – 110 017, India • Penguin Group (NZ), 67 Apollo Drive,
Rosedale, North Shore 0632, New Zealand (a division of Pearson New Zealand Ltd.) •
Penguin Books (South Africa) (Pty.) Ltd., 24 Sturdee Avenue, Rosebank, Johannesburg
2196, South Africa

Penguin Books Ltd., Registered Offices: 80 Strand, London WC2R 0RL, England

First published by Plume, a member of Penguin Group (USA) Inc. Previously
published in a Hudson Street Press edition.

First Plume Printing, March 2008
10 9 8 7 6

ⓟ REGISTERED TRADEMARK—MARCA REGISTRADA

The Library of Congress has catalogued the Hudson Street Press edition as follows:
Brodey, Denise.
    The elephant in the playroom : ordinary parents write intimately and honestly
about the extraordinary highs and heartbreaking lows of raising kids with special
needs / Denise Brodey.
        p. cm.
    ISBN 978-1-59463-035-4 (hc.)
    ISBN 978-0-452-28908-6 (pbk.)
    1. Children with disabilities—Family relationships.   2. Parents of children with
disabilities.   3. Parenting.   I. Title.
    HQ773.6.B75   2007
    306.874087—dc22   2006039393

Printed in the United States of America
Set in Garamond

A PLUME BOOK

THE ELEPHANT IN THE PLAYROOM

DENISE BRODEY is the editor in chief of *Fitness* magazine. She lives in Brooklyn with her two children, Emily and Toby, and her husband, Jeff. And their lizard, Geico. And their dog, Bailey. Her writing has appeared in *The New York Times, O, The Oprah Magazine, Glamour, Self*, and *Child*.

A *Library Journal* Best Book of 2007

"To read the stories of ordinary-turned-extraordinary parents inspires awe and wonder. . . . In this admirably compiled collection, dozens of courageous and eloquent parents show us how to be."
—Carol Kranowitz, author, *The Out-of-Sync Child*

"By sharing the experiences of those who have grappled with the raw and often harrowing feelings that arise from raising children with all types of physical, emotional, and learning obstacles, Denise Brodey offers parents much-needed reassurance that they are not alone in their struggle. . . . *The Elephant in the Playroom* is a celebration of spirit, a source of inspiration, and a testament to how parents rise to challenging situations and learn to appreciate their children's unique, lovable differences." —Miriam Arond, editor in chief, *Child*

"Until the day when every baby is born healthy, it's vitally important for parents to be informed and be connected with others in similar circumstances. Denise Brodey performs a great service for the special-needs community letting parents know they are not alone in their struggles."
—Dr. Jennifer L. Howse, president, March of Dimes Foundation

"Heartbreakingly sad, unexpectedly funny, and always honest. Parents of special-needs kids often feel isolated and criticized; in these pages, they will find a wise and understanding community . . . An original and helpful addition to the parenting shelf."

—*Library Journal* (starred review)

"What a gift this book is for parents. . . . Denise Brodey's collection brings comfort, advice, hope, and inspiration for the parents, grandparents, and teachers of special-needs children who often worry and struggle alone. *The Elephant in the Playroom* should be required reading for anyone who cares about kids."

—David Walsh, Ph.D., author, *Why Do They Act That Way?*

This book is dedicated to my grandparents
Laura and Reuben Rapport.

Acknowledgments

This book was a giant group effort, and it is only because of the courageous parents who wrote about their most private battles—and Danielle Friedman and Laureen Rowland at Hudson Street Press, who saw the collective value in their stories—that this essay collection even exists. I cannot thank all of you enough. Of course, many of these essays would not have landed on my desk if it had not been for the efforts of Erica Rex, researcher extraordinaire. She coaxed the details from harried parents and talked the most Nervous Nellie writers into spilling their guts. Her year of tireless work online, on the phone, and on paper is much appreciated.

I also need to thank my agent, Kate Lee, at ICM in New York. From the minute she heard my idea for this book, she was a fan. We met while I was still at *Glamour*, but I think she knew before I did that I was destined to leave and write my heart out. And, of course, I did, while my parents and in-laws and best friends, including my dearest Katherine, took care of the details of my family life—feeding the lizard, watching the dog, entertaining cranky children. When my husband was playing Mr. Mom, which he does quite well, you were there for him. Thank you.

Of course, Emily and Toby, my glorious, amazing children, are always my inspiration. Their pride and patience and willingness to let me tell their stories is priceless and rare. I owe most of their fabulousness to my husband. I also want to thank my parents and my brother for making "quirky" cool and showing me that being called "weird" can be a compliment.

And Ellen: Don't think I don't remember that night at *Glamour* when you thought of the title for this book—*The Elephant in the Playroom*. It's perfect. And, of course, thank you for taking time out from editing copy about mascara and relationships for me whenever I needed a phone to scream into. You're the best, as are the friends who have stuck by me through thick and thicker: Rebecca, Jill P., Stan, Terri and Eric, and my two surrogate moms, Hilda and Barbara.

Contents

Section 3
The Roller Coaster 81

Section 4
Schools That Work, Schools That Don't 111

Section 5
To Medicate or Not to Medicate 145

Section 6
Going Public   **173**

Section 7
Seeing the Forest Through the Trees **199**

Terms to Know

ADD: Attention deficit disorder is a condition that is characterized by an individual's inability to focus and concentrate on a task; typical behavior includes fidgeting and inattentiveness. ADD can also affect social relationships and self-esteem.

ADHD: Attention deficit hyperactivity disorder can manifest itself in impulsivity and inattention that is not developmentally appropriate. Children with ADHD often experience difficulty at home and in school and with peer relationships. ADHD has also been shown to have long-term adverse effects on school, work, and social-emotional success.

Anxiety: A physical and emotional response to real or imagined danger; symptoms can include increased heart rate, altered breathing, temporary trembling, and difficulty sleeping. Types of anxiety disorders include separation anxiety, phobias, and social anxiety.

Descriptions are based on information from the following organizations: American Academy of Family Physicians (familydoctor.org), American Academy of Child and Adolescent Psychiatry (www.aacap.org), U.S. Department of Health and Human Services Substance Abuse and Mental Health Services Administration (www.mentalhealth .samhsa.gov), American Psychiatric Association (www.psych.org), National Institute of Mental Health (www.nimh.nih.gov), Medicine.net, and the Sensory Processing Disorder Network (www.SPDNetwork.org).

Asperger's Syndrome: Asperger's syndrome is a type of pervasive developmental disorder (see p. xvi) that involves delays in the development of basic skills, including socializing, coordination, and the ability to communicate. Although it is sometimes similar to autism, children diagnosed with Asperger's usually have higher-functioning intelligence and language skills.

Autism: Autism is a pervasive developmental disorder, a group of illnesses that involve delays in the development of basic skills, including the ability to socialize, use imagination, and communicate. Children on the autism spectrum may have trouble bonding with parents and family members, and have problems understanding the world around them and may appear to be atypically self-absorbed.

Bipolar Disorder: Previously referred to as manic depressive illness, bipolar disorder is characterized by cycles of mania (euphoria), alternating with bouts of depression. Since symptoms are often confused or concurrent with other conditions, this disorder is frequently diagnosed later in life. Many who suffer from bipolar disorder also have behavioral and mental difficulties.

Cardiomyopathy: Cardiomyopathy is a condition in which the muscle of the heart is abnormal for unknown reasons. There are four types of cardiomyopathy: hypertrophic (HCM), dilated (DCM), restrictive (RCM), and arrhythmogenic right ventricular (ARVC).

Cerebral Palsy (CP): A group of motor problems and physical disorders related to brain injury. CP causes uncontrolled reflex movements and muscle tightness, and may cause a disturbed sense of balance and depth perception. Several conditions, such as mental retardation, seizures, or vision and hearing problems, are also associated with cerebral palsy.

Depression: A mental illness that experts say is characterized by deep sadness, feelings of guilt, and sometimes a tendency toward suicide. Children under stress, who experience loss, or who have attention, learning, conduct, or anxiety disorders are at a higher risk for depression. Depression tends to be hereditary.

Hydrocephalus: Hydrocephalus is an abnormal accumulation of cerebrospinal fluid (CSF) within the ventricle cavities inside the brain. Hydrocephalus that is congenital (i.e., present at birth) is thought to be caused by a complex interaction of environmental and genetic factors. It is believed to occur in about one in five hundred individuals.

Noonan Syndrome: A genetic disorder that causes abnormal development of many body parts, particularly the webbing of the neck and chest. It affects at least one in twenty-five hundred children, according to the National Institutes of Health.

Obsessive-Compulsive Disorder (OCD): OCD is an anxiety disorder that presents itself as recurrent, persistent obsessions or compulsions. Obsessions are intrusive ideas, thoughts, or images that are often unrealistic or irrational. Compulsions are repetitive behaviors or mental acts that one feels he or she must complete.

Oppositional Defiant Disorder (ODD): When a child defies authority by disobeying, talking back, arguing, or being uncooperative and hostile in a way that is excessive compared to typically developing children—and this pattern of behavior continues for more than a period of six months—it is often termed ODD. Many children and teens with ODD also often have other behavioral problems, such as ADHD, learning disabilities, and mood and anxiety disorders.

Panic Disorder: According to the American Academy of Child and Adolescent Psychiatry (AACAP), this treatable disorder occurs in both children and adults, and includes repeated periods of intense fear or discomfort along with a racing heart and feeling of shortness of breath that can last minutes to hours. These attacks may develop without warning. More than 3 million Americans experience panic disorder, which can be hereditary.

Pervasive Developmental Disorders: A class of mental disorders that begin in infancy (symptoms typically appear before the child is three years old) and are characterized by disordered development in several areas, including social skills and language.

Reactive Attachment Disorder: This disorder usually begins in children under the age of five and can be associated with separation, neglect, or abandonment by birth parents or other caregivers, and/or with physical, psychological, or sexual trauma, or emotional abuse.

Schizophrenia: This mental illness is characterized by a disconnect between cognition and emotion; by disturbances in form and content of thought, mood, and sense of self (including loss of boundaries between reality and dreaming, confused thinking, social withdrawal, and odd or eccentric activity or inactivity).

Selective Mutism: This is a social phobia characterized by a child's inability to speak in select settings. (Children with this disorder do, however, understand language and speak normally in comfortable, secure surroundings.)

Sensory Processing Disorder (SPD): A complex brain disorder that affects adults and developing children. This disorder causes patients to misinterpret everyday sensory information like movement, sound, and touch. They may seek out intense sensory experiences, feel overwhelmed by information, or have other, varying symptoms, according to the Sensory Processing Disorder Network.

Tardive Dyskinesia: A neurological syndrome caused by long-term use of neuroleptic drugs, which are generally prescribed for psychiatric disorders, as well as for some neurological or gastrointestinal disorders. Tardive dyskinesia causes the body to perform recurring, unintentional, purposeless movements, often including quick eye blinking, grimacing, tongue protrusion, lip smacking or puckering, as well as rapid movements of the arms, fingers, and legs, according to the National Institute of Mental Health.

Tourette's Syndrome: Tourette's syndrome includes multiple motor and one or more vocal tics, which occur many times per day, nearly daily. If a child has Tourette's, symptoms tend to appear from three to ten years old.

Turner's Syndrome: This rare genetic disorder affects females and is characterized by the absence of an X chromosome. Characteristics include short stature, retarded development of sexual characteristics, low hairline, and abnormal eye and bone development.

the
elephant
in the
playroom

A View from Within the Whirlwind

My four-year-old son, Toby, was spinning like a top, howling, and we were all just going about our business as if there was nothing extraordinary going on in the living room. This was typical—by this, I mean the "ignoring him" part was pretty much routine. After months of practice, my husband and even my six-year-old daughter could watch Toby lose it and still continue on with our day-to-day lives. It's not that we weren't moved or shaken—we'd just seen this happen *Groundhog Day*–style one too many times.

I was waiting out the storm in the hall, tying my daughter's shoes. We were getting ready to go to a friend's barbecue. I yelled to my husband, Jeff, who was in the kitchen, "Bring a milk in the backpack and make sure you have a sippy cup and Motrin in there, too. You know how Toby gets a headache when he's in a loud group." I heard the *kathunk* of my husband dropping the supplies in the backpack and letting out an exhausted grunt. I must have grimaced, because my daughter asked me, "What's wrong, Mommy?"

I have no idea what my response to her was that day, but I remember what went through my mind: *What's WRONG? Your little brother is throwing a hissy fit for the umpteenth time today. His behavior is unmanageable. We have tried time-outs, rewards, behavior*

*charts—everything. And did you know Mommy and Daddy's mar-
riage is hanging by a thread?*

I normally look forward to spring the way some people look forward to Christmas. I love the season of bike rides and park picnics
and meeting the ice cream truck after dinner. But May 2003 was not
the same. I was not in the mood for Mister Softee—or anything else,
for that matter. I was in a foul state of mind.

Over the past few months I had become a bundle of nerves.
Nothing I'd read about raising a kid told me how to deal with *this*.
Toby's hour-long, completely unpredictable tantrums made me feel
anxious, like a bad mother, a helpless failure. And *everything* seemed
to set him off: I described him to my best friend as a mini–control
freak with a mighty rage. Daily, sometimes hourly, his need to control people and his surroundings disrupted our lives. And that spring,
starting with the first barbeque of the season, would mark a turning
point. That weekend I realized that the problem was bigger than Jeff
and me, that we needed professional help.

Once Toby's tantrum finally ran its course a half-hour later, we
wiped away his tears, had a cold drink, and started off for the barbeque. When we arrived at my friend Ellen's home, Toby studied her
kitchen. I could see his mind ticking: *What are those weird cooking
smells? What are they going to make us eat for dinner?* He checked
out the gaggle of kids playing tag and ball in the garden below. *Too
chaotic*, I bet he thought. So he wandered inside and poked around
with a set of colorful magnetic letters on the fridge. Seconds later, a
precocious preschooler zoomed into the kitchen. I cringed, realizing
he was headed straight for the refrigerator. He screamed, "Toby! I can
spell *Toby!*" and grabbed the letter *O* from my son's fist. I leaned in
and tried to explain to the other child how much Toby wanted to
spell his own name. My friend stopped her cooking to watch me out
of the corner of her eye, with a look that said, *Denise, don't interfere.*

I tried not to, but a duel for the *O* was already under way. Finally, Toby relinquished his letter—but not without a monster tantrum. Other moms chatted and cut cheese wedges and poured wine and tried to ignore the chaos beside them. When Toby refused to be quieted, I took him to the bathroom. He continued hollering into the toilet, telling me he was going to throw up. I took him outside to a quiet front step. He wailed and pounded me with his fists. Through the glass door behind us, I made hand signals to my husband that I was leaving. He cracked open the door and tossed me our house keys. We headed up the block. Toby stumbled and kicked and fell and whined as I cajoled him, distracted him, told him that I loved him. But I can honestly say, at that moment, I couldn't have hated him more. (I am guessing that I am not alone in having this love-hate feeling—while I always deeply love my kids, I can absolutely loathe their behavior and their presence when they push me too far.) I felt confused and furious and so frustrated that I kicked a rock, hard, and stubbed my little toe. Focusing on the throbbing inside my sneaker felt better than dealing with my raging son. I went to sleep with a pain in my foot and an even bigger ache in my heart.

The next day, a Sunday, was no better than the day of the barbeque. By midafternoon, we'd argued over getting dressed, brushing teeth, bike riding in the rain (not an option, I told him), and everything else in between. Every transition was either cause for a battle or a tantrum or both. During our final afternoon argument, Toby again fell on the floor sobbing. My husband gave me a look from the doorway of Toby's room that mirrored my own thoughts: *What the heck was going on with this kid?*

Parents I've told this first-barbeque-weekend story to usually fall into two camps: Camp A would be the "And What the Heck Is Wrong with Your Parenting Skills?" group. These parents are raising kids who have tantrums but accept discipline. These parents pat themselves on the back when their child learns a lesson within a reasonable amount of time and stops the nonsense. Don't get me wrong—members of this group offer well-meaning, constructive advice and commentary: *Maybe more routines would help? Is he feeling sick? What if you . . .* But I'd heard and tried these tactics before; my firstborn was a kid who actually *got* the behavior rulebook in utero and stuck to it most of the time. Camp B, the "We Feel Your Pain" group, on the other hand, can see, almost instinctively, this is no ordinary kid. These parents are almost all moms and dads of special-needs kids. They know life within the whirlwind.

I couldn't stand to struggle with my son like this any longer—or to see the rest of my family take a mental beating, either. A few weeks after the barbeque incident (and many subsequent others), my feelings of hopelessness and stress propelled me to get help—for me and for Toby. A few weeks after that, in late June, a psychologist diagnosed my son with sensory integration dysfunction. She was not the first therapist we consulted—but her observations struck a chord with us. They seemed sensible, fitting. We went with her diagnosis, which in layman's terms means that Toby is highly sensitive to light, noise, sound, and touch, and has problems with learning, organizing his thoughts, and behaving appropriately when his senses are overwhelmed. She sent us to a psychiatrist, Dr. Nieder, who said that the anxiety that all these problems produce led him to believe that Toby also suffers from childhood depression. He prescribed Prozac.

While the idea of giving Toby antidepressants was difficult for me, it was extremely depressing to my husband. Jeff was dubious about medicating a child—but he was also overwhelmed, which made him more open to the idea of Prozac combined with therapy. Jeff's response to trauma had always been: Be silent, wait it out. In the months leading up to Toby's diagnosis, whenever I told Jeff I thought we were in crisis mode and needed help, he would get this shell-shocked deer-in-the-headlights look that is usually reserved for walking in on your wife cheating with the plumber. I did finally get it out of him that he was willing to try Toby on medication, but that was about it. As we began couples and child therapy, Jeff could see the benefits of talking out conflicts and sorting through feelings; he did a lot less silent brooding and displayed fewer looks of horror and shock, although, to this day, listening, not talking, is his forte.

My parents, on the other hand, are talkers *and* listeners—they're both therapists. So when things got especially hellish that pivotal summer, I often turned to them to vent. But we were all so busy. Remembering to call at exactly five of the hour (when my parents were free between patients) or after bedtime, when I could barely form a sentence, proved nearly impossible. It was also draining to try to explain my reality to people who weren't living it themselves.

Before, during, and in the months following Toby's diagnosis, I had never felt so alone. Out of that desperate loneliness came the idea for this book. I wanted to know how other parents of not-so-normal kids made it through the day. I craved real moms' and dads' opinions, solutions, setbacks, and successes. So I began asking a few insightful parents of quirky, less-than-average kids—acquaintances from around the neighborhood I'd gotten to know over the years—to write out their stories for me in an e-mail. As I read each one, I was riveted. Sure, we'd talked "issues" casually at birthday parties, but, *wow*, there was so much in their stories that was, honestly, shocking to read. Being privy to the details of what other special-needs parents go through daily provided a kind of comfort that I hadn't found in books or friends with less quirky kids. I suspected other parents would benefit from hearing these stories as well.

I am a magazine editor, and unearthing compelling stories about real people is what I have done for the past fifteen years. Inspired by the few stories moms and dads that I knew had sent to me, I decided to put my professional skills to the task and expand my search to a broader network of parents. I began my hunt by inviting contributions from those who logged on to special-needs Web sites; then I

posted flyers and did mass mailings to special-needs schools and programs across the country. I put out feelers to respected national asso-
ciations, including the National Institute of Mental Health, Yale Child
Study Center, and the Schwab Learning Organization. I tapped into
psychologists and occupational therapy practices across the country. I
asked for essays that were short, honest, and personal, and could in
some way be helpful to other parents. I suggested topics, including the
stresses of parenting, school dilemmas, the trials and triumphs of giving a child medication, the ways in which a special-needs child had affected a marriage or friendship, and the unexpected joys of being a
mom or dad to a kid who poses certain challenges. I suggested these
topics because they were the ones I felt most in need of hearing about.
But I was very open to ideas; I ultimately wanted this book to be about
what no one was talking about—hence, the title, *The Elephant in the
Playroom*.

The reception from those initial parents, educators, and therapists
I contacted was overwhelmingly positive; many wrote back enthusiastically, in support of the idea—and many wanted to contribute. Inspired by this initial feedback, I expanded my outreach even further,
contacting dozens more therapists, neuropsychologists, child-study
centers, and online special-needs communities. My calls for stories
brought in contributions from ordinary moms and dads hailing from
Florida to Alaska, all of whom were raising kids with extraordinary
challenges, including ADD, ADHD, autism, bipolar disorder, schizophrenia, selective mutism, oppositional disorder, and everything in
between. While I occasionally encountered some resistance, the nas-
tiest comments zapped back at me asked why I would even think of
taking advantage of vulnerable parents for my own gratification.
Those people had missed the point: Overwhelmingly, contributors
gave selflessly of their time and insights because they wanted to help
other parents. Many said they found the writing itself therapeutic.
Others commented in e-mails that putting their family's story into

words had sharpened their focus, helping them hone in on a problem. This nation of parents, it seemed, was ready to talk.

My research also proved to me that there were *a lot* of these parents. Nearly 5 percent, or an estimated 2.7 million children, are reported by their parents to suffer from definite or severe emotional difficulties,* and the World Health Organization indicates that by the year 2020 childhood neuropsychiatric disorders will rise by over 50 percent.† Fifteen percent of parents with children between the ages of five and eighteen report giving their kids psychoactive medication daily for those special needs.‡ During the spring that I began writing, a landmark medical study showed that more than 46 percent of Americans suffer a mental disorder during their lifetime, and many receive inadequate treatment. Autism made the cover of *Time*. And every day that I read the news, it seemed that a new study was surfacing that acknowledged the "hidden handicap" of mental illness was on the rise in children in this country.

How to Use This Book

In this collection you'll find essays by real moms, dads, and even a few siblings—essays full of honest, engaging, eye-opening stories from people who know life in the trenches. You can read the collection from cover to cover, or pick and choose from a section that peaks your interest or is particularly relevant to you. This book covers topics that often get brushed under the rug—emotional topics, like the guilt or confusion involved in giving your child medication

---

America's Children: Key National Indicators of Well-Being, 2005. See www.child stats.gov/amchildren05/index.asp.

†The Executive Summary, Report of the National Advisory Mental Health Council's Workgroup on Child and Adolescent Mental Health Intervention Development and Deployment.

‡New York University Child Study Center. See also "Finding What Works," www.msnbc.com/id/7528650/site/newsweek.

and the frustration with friends who don't understand your parenting style. Unlike diagnostic books, in this collection you will not find expert opinions or checklists for assessing your child's disorder. And you will not find case studies or a blow-by-blow of how and why kids are diagnosed with mental illness. Instead, you will read about ground less covered: pages of parents' perspectives and feelings.

You'll read about the experiences of a four-year-old girl from Texas who told her mom she wished she could make herself go away forever, and of a teenage girl hell-bent on meeting older men on the Internet as a way to ease her loneliness. There is a contribution from an Indiana mom who nearly took her own life when the special needs of her child overwhelmed her. You will also meet Nadine, a New Jersey mother whose son's major issues have always centered on food. The day when this athletic little boy decides to try a new food, even something as simple as chicken nuggets, is one of celebration. You'll find the moving story of a father who upended his entire life to care singlehandedly for a baby born with severe disabilities. These eye-opening stories are not meant to scare or outrage parents; they simply bring a real voice to the epidemic of childhood mental illness that has just begun to show up in statistics and studies.

How This Book Is Different

I am not a therapist. I do not have a degree in early-childhood education, nor have I ever worked at an accredited day-care or a child-study center. I am an editor at a national women's magazine, and I am a reporter, a digger of facts and stories by nature. I understand different diagnoses because I have read several diagnostic "what to do if"–type books—from *The Difficult Child* to *The Out-of-Sync Child*—while trying to comprehend my child's behavior, and I am grateful to the authors who wrote them. But, again, this book is not meant to be diagnostic. I think we can all gain as much knowledge from parents as we do from professionals.

You probably picked up this book in part because you already believe that every child is unique and that the way every child is affected by a disorder varies. The goal of this collection is not to give generalized advice on these disorders, but to provide a source of solace, connection, and community to moms and dads raising special-needs kids. Parents of children who do not have special challenges often rely on peers and the culture they see around them as a guide to raising their families. Special-needs parents, however, watch their children's behavior and challenges morph so quickly that parenting them demands new inspiration almost daily. Not to mention, finding other special-needs parents in some areas is not so easy. The nearest special school or playgroup is often hours away.

Finally, I need to confess that in the last couple of months of working on this book, I've felt like an imposter. Back in the days when I conceptualized this book, my life was truly a disaster. Today my son seems every bit a success story—and his special needs, particularly his anxiety, can go undetected to the naked eye many days. But it has been quite a haul to get where we are (or, I should say, he is) today. For whatever reason you have this book in your hand, I hope that these original works, penned by other concerned, insightful, and wonderful parents all across the country, provide that feeling of connectedness and community I know so many of us need.

SECTION 1

Think Different

When I first realized that Toby was about as quirky as they come, and I noticed my daughter, Emily, noticing this also, I stressed over how I was going to explain their differences—both to each other and to outsiders.

As I write this, my daughter—who is kind, sensitive, straightforward, and decidedly mainstream—is lying beside me reading a chapter book called, fittingly, *All Alone in the Universe*. She is nine years old now, and I ask her if she remembers how I explained Toby's disabilities to her a few years back. She stares at my computer screen. She's ready—I can see from the look on her face that she's been hoping I'd ask for her input on this book. She says, "I remember you told me that Toby can't handle more than one thing at a time. Like if you say, do you want chocolate ice cream, and then someone changes the subject to say, what did you do at school, he'll get confused." True, I had explained that Toby has trouble thinking like other people. I smile that she remembers this. She adds earnestly, "You also said it will not always be easy for me to have him as a brother."

These truthful talks have always helped our family: They establish the facts. They explain how to deal with the realities. They show that Jeff and I have zero tolerance for secrets. This attitude has become liberating—for me, for Jeff, for Emily, and for Toby. These days, we don't shy away from being eccentric. We chat about how, sometimes, being quirky can be embarrassing—or how it can be fun. At dinner a few weeks ago, I asked the kids to name things that made us different from other families. They told me: We talk to our dog about our feelings! We dump all the toys on the floor and organize them, and you call it a Dumparooni! We do yoga at night together to calm down. Yes, it's true, when I take a step back and look at us, Jeff and I do use some pretty unconventional means of parenting—yoga before bed, sorting and reorganizing the kids' stuff by first dumping all of their toys like scrap metal in a central heap. Many days, we enjoy what's called "the one-minute scream"—we get all our anger out at once and then, trust me, we get quiet. But these are things we do in private.

While we may get a kick out of being quirky at home—we may even pride ourselves on being quirky individuals—we still suffer under the unrelenting pressure to be "normal" in the outside world. On the playground, until very recently, I was the mom explaining to another child that Toby doesn't like when others touch him. I'd often tell them Toby had a "space bubble" around him (this proved to be the most compelling explanation), then tiptoe around him in the shape of a circle, pointing and poking at the imaginary bubble. When well-meaning waiters and grocery store clerks tried to talk to Toby, I'd have to wave them off—"He's playing the quiet game. You know . . . first one to speak loses," I'd tell them. I did this because I knew he'd scream if anyone but us offered to help him or serve him. This was my way of keeping outsiders at bay without having to explain why.

Parenting is *not* how I imagined it would be—nor, I imagine, how any of us expected it to be. Over the years, however, the best advice I've gotten has been from other harried, worried parents with children just like Toby. Knowledge of how they handled school, playdates, and tantrums was power. It made me feel less weird, more "in tune," and more capable with my special-needs child.

When every day requires thinking different, though, even the most in-tune mom can miss or misread the signs of trouble. In "Hysterical Blindness," Ellen Glaser writes that she convinced herself that her twelve-year-old son, Josh, who was diagnosed with nonverbal learning disorder, was thriving. But when Josh's mind turns against him one day at school, it shows how deeply complicated mental illness is—and the strange ways the mind can revolt when you ignore its cries for help. To help him recover, she needed to think outside the box—to question doctors, and to be unusually open with her son. Focusing solely on his physical symptoms was not the answer.

I quit trying to get Toby (or Emily for that matter) to act like other kids when I started seeing how being unique was more comforting to them. And with each school year, I am witnessing how Toby can recalibrate his own behavior to fit in when he wants to—agreeing to speak in front of the class even though he is terrified, traveling by bus with his class to a baseball game without worrying he is going to be motion sick, even attending birthday parties he would normally have shunned—too loud, too noisy! That does not happen so magically with some kids. And the heartbreak of watching a child falter and become frustrated with himself and others is vividly depicted in "My Other Half" by Lisa Carver, whose son was diagnosed with schizophrenia and bipolar disorder before he turned nine. "I saw kids fighting to not have to sit next to Wolf during circle time. He is impulsive and erratic with his body as well as with his mind. I often had bruises from, say, his arm suddenly whacking backward . . . almost as if jerked by invisible wires. 'He doesn't mean to. He really likes you. He's just a little goofy. Just remind him: Personal space,' I'd tell the kids. . . . They wanted none of it."

Much as a museum guide translates an artist's vision, many parents of special-needs kids become the interpreters of their child's behavior. Nicole Lynch, the mother of an autistic preschooler, says she struggled to describe the feeling of "permanent jet lag" she and her husband experienced because their child would not sleep through the night—even close family had a difficult time understanding what they were going through. It wasn't until this little girl with "sleep issues" stayed with her grandparents that they, too, finally got it—no interpreter needed.

On the flip side, the *children* in this section *taught* their parents a few things about thinking differently as well, particularly when a parent didn't have the time or patience or energy to "see" what their child was trying to say. In short, these stories are bite-size lessons in coping—perfect for times when, as a parent of a special-needs kid, you feel as though you may have bitten off more than you can chew.

What's Not for Lunch

Nadine

Nadine is the mother of Jake,* ten, who struggles with sensory integration issues. She and her family live in a small town in New Jersey.

If Jake knew I was writing this, he'd be heartbroken and confused. As far as he's concerned, there is nothing special about him. He's just a normal ten-year-old boy.

Sometimes I agree. When he's had enough rest and food, he's a sunny, energetic kid. But that well-adjusted child can disappear in a nanosecond if he feels his sense of predictability and safety is in jeopardy. Jake has a very strong sense of "order." If my husband, Steve, or I threaten that, he gets very wound up. Even offering dessert suggestions during a meal can make him anxious and angry. I'm not quite sure how to explain it, but he seems to have a keen sense of what is "right," and he doesn't like us messing with it in any way.

When Jake was young, transitions were very hard, but we coped. We got to parties first so that he could establish a sense of place without having to grapple with new people at the same time. We always reviewed plans for the weekend in advance, so he'd know what to expect.

Today, at ten, transitions are easier for Jake—most of his issues now center on food and clothing. From what I've read, his behavior

*Names have been changed.

in some ways looks a bit like autism. We never got a diagnosis. We just call him highly sensitive, or quirky. In the beginning, his behavior seemed a little odd, but within the range of normal. By the time my husband and I realized that he was on the far end of the bell curve, we decided not to do anything. To this day, I'm not exactly sure why. We consulted lots of specialists, read books and articles, and even tried therapy twice. But Jake was very resistant to professional help, and this made us all miserable, so it seemed easier to work with him ourselves. Maybe it was bad parenting, but I hope not. The truth is, Steve and I know Jake. His quirks have never been too overwhelming, and he gets easier over time.

Then again, when I think about the contortions we've gone through to help Jake, I am amazed that we all haven't fallen apart at the seams yet.

Consider toilet training. He was terrified of the sensation of sitting to poop. Jake was "night trained" before he was "day trained." Peeing in the toilet wasn't a problem because he could stand up to do it. But sitting down to poop was a whole other matter. He'd will himself to make it through a day of preschool without having to go to the bathroom, so he could wear underpants all day like the other kids. Then, later, at home, when he felt his bowels needing to move, he'd ask my husband or me to put on a diaper. He turned four and still insisted on the diaper. We tried to push the matter, but he was good at holding it in. We took him to a therapist, but her strategies were no match for his persistence. By the time he was four and a half, we were nervous he might still be wearing diapers in kindergarten. So we took a do-it-ourselves approach. Over Easter vacation, my husband and I tossed out the diapers and began secretly putting Senacot (a laxative) into his milk. When the Senacot finally became too much for him, the bathroom scene was heart-wrenching: He screamed. He kicked. He cried, "Just buy me a diaper!" He was like a drug addict in need of a fix. But we stuck to our guns and physically held him down on the potty until he finally let it out. Within a few days, he was using the toilet like a pro. Problem solved.

Jake's issues with clothing have also caused us our fair share of agita over the years. Like a lot of kids, he has to remove tags because they're itchy. But he's also picky about "what feels right." He wouldn't wear blue jeans until kindergarten and wore a button-down shirt for the first time only last month. Throughout pre-K he insisted on stretch-waist blue twill pants with a solid red long-sleeve shirt. That's all he would wear, every day.

The major problem, though, has always been food. Jake is an athletic kid, and he needs a fair amount of fuel to keep going. His extremely limited diet—cheddar cheese (extra-sharp only), crackers, bagels, cereal, and fluorescent-colored yogurt products—combined with his reluctance to try new foods makes keeping him fed an incredible challenge. Getting him to eat a peanut butter sandwich when he was seven years old took six months and countless tiny baby steps. First, we had a chocolate taste test (yes, the kid does love chocolate). Hoping that Jake would go for the taste of peanut butter mixed with chocolate, we chose seven candy bars. One was a Reese's Peanut Butter Cup. Bingo. A few weeks later, we tried dipping some chocolate into creamy peanut butter. Again, acceptable. We were one step closer to getting his taste buds acquainted with a peanut butter sandwich. Knowing he had successfully tried Ritz Crackers in the past, we coaxed him to try Ritz peanut butter crackers. Another win. Steve and I were doing victory dances in the living room. Then we tried a peanut butter sandwich on toast, cut into small circles exactly the size of the Ritz (toast looked most like Ritz). A few weeks later, we moved on to . . . a plain peanut butter sandwich on full-size bread. He'll eat them now—sometimes. We're in heaven.

I have to confess: We never would have gotten to peanut butter sandwiches if it hadn't been for Steve. He is just more in sync with the way Jake works. The truth is, I am not very patient when it comes to the slow and steady pace that Jake prefers—I prefer to jump right in. Early on, I put aside any "mother knows best" preconceived notions and recognized that when it comes to Jake, Steve generally knows best. I learn a lot by watching him parent. I think a lot of moms assume they've got all the knowledge, and their husbands bumble through things. But I've always been clear that when it comes to Jake, I am the "bumbler"; Steve understands the finessing that is needed. So he stops me before I try to push through lots of changes at once and gets me to move more gradually. I did the chocolate taste test with seven brands. Steve cut the peanut butter sandwich on toast into round circles.

When people hear about Jake's food issues, they roll their eyes. Many suggest that we just leave him at their house for the weekend. They figure we're not trying hard enough, or that we give in too easily. But they don't know Jake, whose anxiety about food is stronger than hunger. In fact, hunger just makes him less able to try new foods. We joke that when Jake was made, he got dealt twice the normal number of taste buds. It's his job to turn them off, one at a time. I was stunned recently, when he rejected a cheddar cheese that he had been eating every day for four years. He said this one felt funny and tasted different. Turns out he was right; by mistake, we had bought cheddar made with 2 percent milk. Unfortunately, the sensitivity is not just in his mouth. He has refused to sit in the kitchen when it smells "bad." "Bad" may be a strong odor like the cumin of Indian food, but it can also be the smell of white rice or plain pasta. I can only trust that there is, indeed, a smell, even if it is only detectable by my son and a bloodhound. But for all our struggles, there are incredible moments. Like when he was eight years old and declared one day that he thought he would try Chicken McNuggets. He liked them so much that I found myself encouraging my child to go to McDonald's as often as possible just to get in a little protein. He rejected Wendy's and Burger King Tenders because they had pepper on them. Still, we had a place to stop on long car trips. Amazingly, he is now able to eat at road stops across America.

The good thing is that once he adds something to his repertoire—blue jeans at age five, chicken nuggets at eight, boogie boarding at nine—he embraces it fully. And after each new addition, he'll begin to refer to himself with the phrase "I'm that kind of kid that . . ." When I hear these statements, momentarily, I'm amazed. How much coaxing and hard work did it take to get him to try these things? And then I just feel proud. Because he's right. He has become "that kind of kid."

You Can't Rush a Good Thing

Lorie Bricker

Lorie Bricker is the mother of Alec, a seven-year-old diagnosed with autism. She lives in Troy, Ohio.

If there's one thing I've learned about raising a child with special needs, it's that sometimes the transformations you are hoping for happen when you least expect them. In the meantime, you should find a way to appreciate your child—always—no matter how challenging life gets. Pretty soon, you will not only begin to understand but will even embrace the differentness of your special-needs child.

My son Alec was diagnosed with autism around the age of five. In the months leading up to his diagnosis, my husband and I had begun picking up on things that bothered us about our otherwise high-functioning kid: He had a few odd behaviors, such as his need to control where he sat, or his resistance to taking even the simplest advice. And because his social skills were pretty poor, he had few friends. He also didn't process information—how or when to do something basic—the way his older brother, Andrew, did.

Part of me knew there was something wrong with Alec, but it wasn't until we relocated to a small town in Ohio (from the larger city of Columbus) and I left my corporate job to be a stay-at-home mom that I had the opportunity to tackle the puzzle of my son's behavior for myself. For the first time in his life, Alec wasn't being subjected to hours of day care, where he was completely misunderstood and always being placed in time-out. I was able to spend more time developing and implementing a daily routine for Alec—when we would eat, play, bathe, and sleep.

When I was a working career mom, I never took or had the time to invest in a routine geared specifically toward benefiting my children. Once I did, I was shocked by how simple changes in our daily life had such an extraordinarily positive impact on my son.

Before I quit my job, my husband and I were always running late to wherever we were going, usually as a result of Alec. In the morning, for example, the more we rushed or yelled for Alec to hurry, the slower he would inevitably go. The fast pace at which we were moving, combined with the excess noise of doors slamming and people shouting for him to get going, get dressed, brush his teeth, and get his coat on, caused him to simply shut everything out. Because he couldn't process all the incoming information, he got lost in the words and would just stay put and ignore everything. Assuming he was just being stubborn, I would become aggravated—I would nudge him along and yell some more. The vicious cycle repeated over and over again, every morning—for years.

After we moved, however, our morning pace slowed, and as it did, Alec seemed better able to transition from one task to another with very little prompting from me. The less prompting, the more at ease he seemed, and the easier it was for him to get dressed on time. Being ready on time automatically eased my frustration, so I stopped yelling at him. Within weeks, we had reversed the cycle. Mornings were a time of quiet togetherness that we actually looked forward to.

With hindsight, I realize that when I worked, in addition to mishandling our morning routine, I had never taken the time to understand the idiosyncrasies that helped Alec feel comfortable in his surroundings. Odd behaviors, such as positioning his chair at the dinner table so that none of the chair legs were touching a grout line between the ceramic tiles, opening the cabinet door on the entertainment center and leaving it open whenever he watched TV, eating his cereal with a specific spoon every morning—all seemed like time wasters. None of his rituals ever made any sense to me, so I would find myself frustrated and impatient. Just sit down and eat! Watch TV without the cabinet door hanging wide open! Use any old spoon that I pulled out of the drawer, please! I still don't understand some of my son's quirks, but it is his routine, and I recognize the comfort value of it.

A few weeks after I began life as a stay-at-home mom, I began noticing a theme in Alec's behavior: In general, the more at ease he was in his surroundings, the less he said *No* and *I don't want to*. His constant defiance, which for years would get us into screaming matches with each other several times a day, waned. Don't get me wrong—some of his habits were harder to break. For months, if I asked him to pick up his toys, he would, without fail, tell me *No*. I'd respond with a *Yes you will!* and he'd shoot back another *No*. This push and pull would last several minutes, and it always ended with Alec in a full-blown meltdown, retreating to his room with a door slam and screaming *I hate you!* as loud as he could. I'd cry, too, in the privacy of my room. I desperately wanted to understand how to communicate with my son and stop feeling like such a failure as a mother.

But then, one day, after I asked Alec to clean his room, and he re-sponded with his typical *No*, I decided to try a different approach: I did not fuel the fire with a retaliatory response. Instead, I said and did nothing. I just waited and observed him for a few minutes. The waiting wasn't easy, but it was worth it. Pretty soon he looked up, as if he had no idea that I was even there, much less that I had just asked him to do something. With his focus on me, he said, "What did you want, Mom?" I calmly repeated my request, and he replied, "Okay," and began to clean up his room. After several days of im-plementing this new stop-wait-don't-engage-him technique, I sud-denly understood the problem: Alec was not able to process what I said at the same rate as other people. When Alec was telling me *No*, he really was just saying, *Give me a minute to process that*. This revelation put a stop to almost two straight years of screaming matches between Alec and me, and stamped out my personal anxiety that I was a bad mother. I don't think that I will be winning any Mom of the Year Awards anytime soon, but every day I gain a bit more confidence in my ability to parent my special-needs son more effectively.

Musical Beds

Nicole Lynch

Nicole Lynch, mother of an autistic preschooler, lives in Napa Valley, California.

My five-year-old daughter, Sarah, has had sleep issues ever since she was a young infant with colic. She overcame the colic, but when she was about nine months old, she began waking every night at about two alert and ready to play. Exhausted, my husband and I eventually stopped sitting up with her and would place her between us in our bed. Ah, rest! The minute we put her in bed with us, she'd fall asleep again. We didn't bother moving her. We were wiped out, so the "family bed" seemed like a great solution for everyone.

When children develop typically, they are ready to move from the family bed to their own bed usually by four years old. *Ready*— meaning with encouragement and support, they can make it through the night on their own. This was not the case with our family. At two and a half years old, our daughter was diagnosed with autism. Autistic kids often suffer from poor sleep. When Sarah was about three and a half years old, the night awakenings returned with a vengeance, and there was little we could do to get our daughter back to sleep. The family bed was no longer enough. It seemed like any slight disruption in her day would wind her up and throw her off her sleep schedule. A simple change in her daily routine (like traveling or going to bed late after spending the day with relatives) set her sleep off for a night, oftentimes a series of nights. Typically, she'd wake up anywhere between one and three and stay up until about five the next day, when she'd finally collapse. She'd sleep a couple of hours, and then wake up, full of energy, sometimes manic, and be unable to fall asleep that night until one or so. When she awoke, she'd do outrageous stuff—like stand up in the bed and start singing "That's Elmo's world!" jump out of bed, ask for "Candle, candle!" (She hoards our candles.) She'd then drag her collection of candles in bed, jump on the bed, and ask us to tickle her or ask for a lollipop. We found this tolerable, at best, until the effects of permanent "jet lag" (without having changed a time zone) set in. My husband, an attorney and the breadwinner (who needs to get up in the morning at seven and be able to think straight), needed relief. He simply couldn't function during the day. So about two years ago, he started sleeping in our daughter's antique full-size bed, by himself, with his feet hanging off the end. (People were shorter one hundred years ago.) My daughter and I slept in our bed. About a year ago we "progressed" a bit: My daughter and I started sleeping in her bed (my feet hang off the end this time), and my husband got our own bed back.

This summer, another phase of musical beds ensued. My husband is no longer "permitted" to sleep peacefully. My daughter has been having a great time swimming with her dad. We've been spending his lunch hours and weekends at the local pool, and the two of them have been living it up. She apparently feels such a bond with him that she wants to sleep beside him every night. She manages to do so without our complaints, mostly because, with all the wonderful exercise she gets swimming and walking, her night awakenings have diminished somewhat. Who knows what will happen when school starts up again? New stresses don't sit well with her and generally affect her sleeping patterns.

I also should mention that the extended family is not immune to Sarah-induced sleep deprivation. My mother visited a few weeks ago, and my daughter insisted on sleeping with her. Grandma couldn't resist, but sure enough Sarah woke at three, discovered she was sleeping with her grandmother (a change!), and did not go back to sleep until the next afternoon. At least my mother now has real a taste of our lifestyle and a deeper understanding of what life with an autistic child is like. Last weekend we visited my parents at their home. My daughter first went to sleep with my husband in the guest room, then hopped into my parents' bed, kicking her granddad out. Then after she fell asleep, I brought her back to sleep with her dad. Then she woke up at two, all worked up, and hopped all around the house, visiting everyone. The whole family was bleary-eyed the next day—everyone except my daughter. I know, you're probably thinking, *Why don't they "train" their daughter to sleep in her bed by herself?* Believe me, this has occurred to us; we've read everything out there on the subject. We have tried, and it hasn't worked—yet. The "experts" say to "ride it out." As she grows, and becomes more regulated, her sleep schedule will stabilize. It appears that children with autism go through periods of development when their sleep is off kilter. So, we do what we can. In the meantime, however, if you think you have a solution, you are welcome to come to our house and try a night with our daughter.

Impacting the Bottom Line

RW

RW is the mother of B, who is twelve years old and has pervasive developmental disorder (PDD). She lives in South Carolina.

Did your parents ever tell you they meant business? Well, maybe they were on to something! Consider our story:

When my son, B, was young, it was impossible to get him to co-operate, no matter what we tried. Time-outs, threats of harsher punishment—they were all useless. He had a capacity for (what I saw as) misbehavior that would rile me up, and then leave me feeling deflated when he wouldn't obey. I just could not understand his obstinacy—didn't it bother him to see me so visibly upset? I think that sometimes B saw my tensely delivered threats as a joke; other times, it was clear he had simply given up hope that he would ever do anything right, so he gave up trying.

It took me a long time to comprehend the ways that autism impacted B's communication skills—particularly as they applied to his ability to understand what was being asked of him. It was apparent from a young age that he was bright, but this didn't mean that he could tell me what "top" meant, when I told him to put his name at the "top" of the page, or that he could manage to put his clothes away "in" his room, or to "take" his jeans "off." In time, I figured out that, to him, my words sounded like the adult character in the "Peanuts" cartoons: He heard *"Waa-waa-waa jeans, B!"* Autism made his need to "visualize" language paramount; the only words whose meaning he understood were nouns. I eventually began to realize that many of his negative behaviors were no more than misunderstandings of what I really wanted of him—or my misunderstandings of what he was capable of doing. How can you obey when you don't know what is being asked of you? In retrospect, I suspect that I was often the problem at these times, not B.

As his language picked up, around age four, B's ability to understand became much better, but it didn't change the fact that he was in opposition, by nature, to many requests made of him. Desperate for a solution, I researched oppositionality on the Internet. I was fascinated to read an actual list of behaviors associated with oppositionality that defined my son to the letter: He was negative, hostile, and defiant; he often lost temper; often argued with adults; refused to comply with adults' requests or rules; deliberately annoyed people; blamed others for his mistakes and misbehavior; was often touchy or easily annoyed by others; was often angry and resentful; was often spiteful or vindictive. Check. Check. Check. The list fit him perfectly. Except for these negativisms, B's behavior was unpredictable, and I was at a loss as to how to deal with it.

He was in third grade when I came across a book called *Ritalin Is Not the Answer*, by psychologist David Stein, which offered an alternative to medication for parents of behaviorally challenging kids. While alternative treatments didn't turn out to be the answer for B, this book gave me valuable insight into the workings of the ADHD/autistic/oppositional mind, namely because of the way B reacted to the "therapy" the book suggested. Over the course of reading *Ritalin Is Not the Answer*, what kept resonating in my mind was Dr. Stein's recommendation to give a child immediate feedback to impulsive behavior. I decided to give it a try.

For two weeks, every time B gave even a hint of noncompliance, my husband and I sat him aside for ten minutes, not allowing him to do a single thing. No TV, no talking—just sitting on the couch. The first night included a whopping twenty-five time-outs. But B quickly got a little more careful, and by the end of two weeks, he had only five or so ten-minute time-outs a night. We were exhausted, though, from the constant surveillance and the constant need to play the role of enforcer. It got to the point where my husband and I were looking for excuses not to punish him. Still, I realized that there were threads to the extreme behavioral plan that I could put into place, without the time and effort it initially involved. Immediate feedback was the clincher.

What I learned by attempting and reading about "immediate feedback" is that many ADD/autistic kids have a profound sense of justice. Being the adult gives you no leeway in their minds. If you ask something of them, you'd better be willing to follow through in your own behavior. If you cuss, you give them permission to also. If you scream and yell, look for it to be a behavior pattern with your child. They hunger for predictability, too. If you say, "No TV until your homework is done," you'd better be willing to back it up every single day, regardless of your plans; otherwise, the threat becomes meaningless, and you have to start from square one.

In addition to his sense of what was fair, B had a keen sense of entitlement, and, as part of my immediate-feedback plan, I had to make it clear to him that before entitlement came responsibility. If you fight with your friends, they have to go home. (We live in an apartment building, which made this easy.) This if-then paradigm gave control to B, by allowing him to make the choice. We figured, if B was going to be naughty, it was going to cost him, not us. There were three things that B coveted most at that age: money, TV time, and getting his way. I ran with the theory that the threat of losing any of those things might coerce good behavior out of him. The plan worked. Broke something in a fit of anger? You'll pay for it with your allowance. Not going to do your homework? Okay, that will cost you TV time. You can go to a friend's house when your chores are done.

No compromises. We *mean business!* Finally, the discipline was stick-ing, and we had a plan we could all live with: If you misbehave, you will pay.

Today I don't have to use idle threats anymore, and B cooperates 90 percent of the time. He knows the rules—and exactly what will happen to him if he breaks them; he gets to decide if misbehaving is worth it. I am, ironically, able to give him a lot more leeway now, be-cause he appreciates the privileges he has and doesn't want to lose them—and somehow, knowing that he is going to cooperate makes me want to increase those privileges. I enjoy being around him now and have found parenting a lot easier since he has had to undergo what I refer to as "cost-benefit analysis" for misbehavior. B has things in his life that he treasures, but in my opinion, these should not be treated as gifts—they are rewards for a job well done. This, and the responsibility that it entails, is something I hope that he can carry with him into adulthood.

Maintaining this system of disciple has been tough, and it some-times doesn't feel like the loving thing to do. But my husband and I have learned that B needs us to lay down clear boundaries so that he can feel safe. B doesn't feel it's unfair because he gets to make his own decisions each day.

Ultimately, I guess my parenting philosophy boils down to this: We all are part of a giant, interdependent circle in this life. Each of us has a part to play at school or work, at home or in public. I want to show B that he needs to do his part, and that everything runs better when he does. Everyone needs to know they are needed. When we make our children responsible, they know they are.

My Other Half

Lisa Carver

Lisa Carver's son was diagnosed as bipolar at age five and schizophrenic at age eight.

He didn't do anything so strange at first. Other four-year-olds talk incessantly about aliens, poop . . . and death—right? Other children hurt animals because they don't know any better, right? I didn't know. I was young. I didn't have other children. I only had my son, Wolfgang. He would learn, I told myself. I talked to him all the time. I explained, I begged. I tried to take empathy and peace out of myself and feed them to him.

Here's what I knew about my child: Doctors had diagnosed Wolf with velocardiofacial syndrome (VCFS), a deletion in chromosome 22. The doctors figured that out when he had heart failure at five days old. They explained to me that there would be speech and swallowing difficulties, motor delays, and learning disabilities. But this was the early 1990s, and not as much was known about the relatively newly discovered VCFS back then, and no one told me that upward of 80 percent of kids with VCFS will develop mental illness such as bipolar disorder and schizophrenia. They said Wolf might never talk. So he and I learned sign language together throughout his toddlerhood—picture these two hearing people hemmed in by our own self-made invisible walls. We created our own signs, too.

At three, he started talking, but our private, constant communications continued. I watched his behavior closely, but it didn't seem like

Wolf was doing anything I'd never had an impulse to do. It was just that with him, impulses became actions instantaneously. He didn't have that split-second vision that would allow a normal person to see the consequences of his actions—and stop in the nick of time. Indeed, after he whacked the cat or yelled at the librarian, he would have no idea why they were angry with him. I would explain, and then he would feel terrible. He would be full of self-hatred. I could never sustain any anger over any ugly, senseless thing he'd done. "I should be dead," he said more than once. "No you shouldn't!" I'd respond, with tears in my eyes. "I'd be brokenhearted." But in a way he was right. Had he been born twenty years earlier, just before some very important advances in infant surgery, he *would* be dead. Perhaps wanting to be dead was a very sane reaction to the amount of pain and confusion Wolfgang had sustained already, in his short time here. Then again, how was I to know that suicidal thoughts were completely out of the ordinary for a four-year-old? Teens frequently entertain morbid thoughts that lead nowhere, and goths in their twenties; why not someone younger when he is as imaginative and dramatic as Wolf?

Because he was so often in the hospital for the first few years of his life—with a gastric tube placement, ear tubes, malrotated intestines rerotated by hand, grueling physical therapy—and so often contagious with some cold or other when he was out, I didn't get to observe him with other children much until he went to preschool. There I saw kids fighting to not have to sit next to Wolf during circle time. He is impulsive and erratic with his body as well as with his mind. I often had bruises from, say, his arm suddenly whacking backward when I was behind him, almost as if jerked by invisible wires. He often had bruises from stumbling into furniture or jumping from places that should not be jumped off of. "He doesn't mean to. He really likes you. He's just a little goofy. Just remind him: 'Personal space,'" I'd tell the kids when I came to pick up Wolf at the end of the day. They wanted none of it.

On the playground, I saw how these children—all a year younger than Wolf—were fluid in their play; they adapted. That's when I realized Wolf could not "switch gears." To this day he will take one role in a game—usually, the monster chasing the others—and cannot restart his engine when it's time to play a new game. He is the monster, forever. It's like that role answers something inside him, some alternate vision. I read that at six years of age, the average kid can pick up around 6,000 social cues. Then there was Wolf at six; he could understand about three cues. I gave him reminders and explanations for the other 5,997. Now, at ten, Wolf's repertoire of interactions has grown some. For example, he sometimes remembers on his own to stop his obsessive listing of conjectures about, say, space aliens, and ask his exhausted conversation partner, "And what do you think?" But he still doesn't really understand what play is. It was, and still is, very *real* to him.

When he started to attend elementary school, other children sensed that realness, and it made them uncomfortable and annoyed. And they were honest. "You can't play with us because you don't know how, Wolf. Go away," one girl said. Wolf just laughed, made more monster growls at her. The teacher told me about this exchange when I came to pick him up, looking like she was about to cry.

At home that night, he cut my husband's arm with a plastic knife, drawing blood. He said, "I'm going to stab you," out of nowhere, and he did. But it wasn't out of nowhere. My husband had been commenting about someone on TV and said, "What a freak!" That was the trigger. That's what the kids on the playground called Wolf. My husband, of course, was furious. I tried to explain it all to him. Then I tried to explain to Wolf why he had done the awful thing he did, and why he could never do that again.

I was—am—a sort of filter between Wolf and the world. I translate Wolf to everybody else, and everybody else to Wolf. I was never successful in showing my husband the secret pathways to the likable parts of my troubled son. He could not understand Wolf or why I would give so much of my life to such a seemingly lost cause. That's most of the reason why we divorced within a few years.

Shortly after the stabbing incident, we got Wolf on a drug his doctors recommended called Zyprexa. It's an antipsychotic, but it's used to treat a host of early-onset mental illness: bipolar disorder, schizophrenia, plain-old psychosis. It worked. The Zyprexa took over a little bit of my job; rather, it allowed me time to do my job with Wolf. As his responses to frustration slowed, I could step in and keep a situation from escalating. And then I had my daughter. When I had only Wolf, I accepted how goddamned hard every little thing is and how it never stopped being hard. But it's not difficult at all to raise Sadie. Whenever I drop the ball on raising her, she picks it up. Not Wolf. He continuously, accidentally smashes the ball from my grip.

At a VCFS conference I attended recently, one of the speakers said something that really stuck with me: He said that as a special-needs kid, you have twenty failures for every success. With "normal" kids, you may experience twenty successes—spontaneous kisses or lessons grasped—for every failure. A meltdown, an inability to fit in or grasp a lesson—these are all considered failures. I came home from the conference and began observing Wolf to a count of twenty— twenty times he would scream instead of using an indoor voice. Twenty times I could not get my shopping done, and we'd end up in the parking lot, both in tears, the full cart abandoned along with one small sandal. The panelists suggested getting out on your own to avoid depression. But how can we do that, when we are like glasses/ hearing aids/leg braces/tour guides for our children? How could I just take away the tools he needed to live? Not until I had Sadie did I realize how inexorably bound Wolf and I are. I am closer to Wolf than I was to my own mother, closer to Wolf than I ever was to my husband or my best friend. Closer even than I am to Sadie. Wolf and I are actually a part of each other. This is forever, I realize now. He is not going to outgrow me. He needs me to complete his thoughts. And I chose to enter his slightly strangled alternate reality so that he wouldn't have to be so all alone in there. Other people, meanwhile, have steadily helped me into isolation. Family, friends, spouse, the person in front of you at the grocery store—they'll tell you he behaves like he does because you are too strict, too lax, too distant, too pampering. They aren't trying to be cruel; they want to help. They're used to children who abide by the Twenty Successes for Every Failure Rule. And you believe them, because you wish it were true. If his behavior were your fault, then you could work to change it. Who wants to believe that there are going to be times when the only way to help your child is to do to him things you wouldn't do to an enemy: physically restrain him, drug him, send him away, even call the police on him. It's unnatural. He's a child. *Your* child. What will happen when I'm gone?

When Wolf was eight or nine, I started taking business trips again. I'd be gone two, three nights. One time he went catatonic on the second day. Other times he does fine. Mostly, he gets physically ill. No fever, but he is lethargic, coughing, even to the point of throwing up. Why? Because a piece of his "self" got up, drove to the airport, and got on a plane. It's hard on me, too, when I leave him. It's not like I exactly enjoy all the extra duties and extra intimacy that parenting a special-needs child entails. But I feel so worried and guilty and unfinished when I'm away from my duties, I often get sick myself on these trips.

I created him, but he created—or re-created—me, too. My son changed me. Every parent says that about every child. But he really changed me. I am happy to allow my daughter space—to spend time with a friend for an hour, to attend preschool, or to be herself, with her private thoughts and private play. Sometimes I'm the strong one, sometimes she is. Our lives move in parallel. We exchange affection and pride in each other, we share experiences, but we are both moving toward our own goals. There will be relationships with others, a life not completely centered on the other. My son, though, is always with me, and I am always in him, even when we are not in the same room. We are and will always be joined, forever.

There were many therapists—for him and for me—and he and I have both learned from them. But after fifty-five minutes, their time with us is over. Our time together never is, even when we're apart. There's so much guilt. Here's something that's hard to admit: I had to forgive him for who he is. Did it turn your stomach to read that sentence? Think of how sickened I must be with myself to have lived that sentence! I, like most people, did not want a "retarded" son. I really didn't. Like most self-taught loners, I valued intellectual agility above all else—maybe even to the exclusion of all else. I wouldn't have minded if my child were physically deformed. But Wolf is clumsy and slow. He walks slowly, he thinks slowly, he even sees slowly. This is probably why he considers himself the savior of all caterpillars—because his eyes are always on the ground and he moves at about the same rate as a caterpillar. When he spies one that has been run over at the side of the road, he cries in a heart-ripping yelp, as if it were he who just got squashed.

This past year has been a very good one for Wolf. But it was very stressful. I was often getting calls from school that he was receiving "messages"—sometimes from aliens, but more often from caterpillars in trouble. They spread the news along their network to migrate to Wolf's house for aid. How could he sit and concentrate on multiplication and cursive when thousands or millions of lives depended on him? He could not! And so I'd drop whatever I was doing and go pick him up. We'd spend the afternoon in the backyard. The sun would shine, or rain would fall softly on us, unnoticed. He seemed happy. We didn't talk. He was one hundred percent focused on his task: to save the fuzzy little creatures from the ravages of the wild, in his terrarium. I'd interrupt him only to feed him, and he'd holler at me the whole time. I had to hold him down and make him take his food. If I didn't, I knew from experience he wouldn't eat for days, until the messages stopped coming.

He will look at books on three topics only: tadpoles turning into frogs, caterpillars turning into butterflies, and molten lava bubbling out of the sea and turning into islands. This boy with a 67 IQ is all about redemption and transformation. I wanted a genius, and it took a long time for me to realize it, but in a peculiar way I got one. He is almost an exaggeration of me: in his own world, with his own bizarre tastes, going his own way. It's just that he needs me to go with him.

Hysterical Blindness

Ellen Glaser

Ellen Glaser is a history professor who lives in Atlanta, Georgia. Josh,* who is twelve years old, has nonverbal learning disorder and has recovered from a bout of hysterical blindness.

Bizarre things happen to parents with special-needs children, but how many can say they lost their child on top of the Empire State Building? For forty-five minutes on an unusually warm winter afternoon three years ago, the entire Observatory staff hunted for my nine-year-old son while his grandmother and I hyperventilated in the gift shop. When they finally brought Josh to us, our grateful tears puzzled him. We shouldn't have been worried, he told us. Unlike his little brother and cousin, he simply hadn't heard us call him to leave. He was trying to find his favorite landmarks thousands of feet below.

You could say this could happen to any kid. Tourists pack the famous site 365 days a year. In my son's case, however, the disappearing act was part of a worrisome pattern. At five, he had gone missing at a synagogue dinner for an hour, and at seven, our local YMCA had to go on lockdown while we frantically searched for him after swim practice. With his wandering ways, I always made sure to purchase a bright coat for him to wear in the winter and neon-hued swimsuits for the summer.

On the other hand, the Empire State Building incident was emblematic of one of Josh's most winning characteristics—his deep cu-

*Names have been changed.

riosity about the world around him, which he pursued relentlessly
and enthusiastically. Given his passion for architecture—back then
he was obsessed with bridges—it's not surprising that he couldn't
pull himself away from the railing of New York's tallest skyscraper.
And that's the way it was with our precious son—intensity and lively
engagement mixed with puzzling lapses in basic functioning. Things
just didn't add up the way they should.

In third grade, for example, Josh brilliantly pulled off an imper-
sonation of Franklin Roosevelt for a class project, reciting excerpts of
the president's famous speeches in a fake upper-class accent. In fourth
grade, perhaps inspired by his hero FDR, he ran for class president on
a platform of "Better school lunches," and he cleverly "hired" several
friends to pose as sunglass-clad Secret Service agents. Every year, he
deepened his dedication to competitive swimming and looked forward to his workouts. Yet, each year, he lost at least a half-dozen
lunch boxes. His homework rarely made it back to school and into his
teacher's hands. Beginning in first grade, his teachers repeatedly told
us that he seemed spacey. We saw him struggling, too. My husband
and I were startled when he was honored at an end-of-the-season
swim team awards ceremony, when he still hadn't learned the names
of all his coaches. His homework would drag on for hours every
night, even though it seemed within the ability of a child whose favorite computer "game" was an architecture-design program. Josh angrily rejected any help from us but continued to argue and cry when
things didn't come easily. Even worse, our bright little boy would
make comments about being "stupid"; teachers grouped him with the
"slow" kids because of his erratic performance.

Although I tried to focus on the positive, by the time Josh entered
fourth grade, my husband and I were losing patience with him, and
that was making things worse. We knew to seek professional assistance, but unfortunately, in our case, we were on the receiving end
of some pretty misguided ideas about how to raise our quirky kid.

We wasted precious time when we failed to trust our intuition and instead let the "experts" brush off our concerns.

My husband and I initially sought aid from a psychologist recommended by our pediatrician. Sitting perched in his wingback chair, while we held hands on the proverbial couch, he delivered his diagnosis. Our son, he told us, was an "F-L-K." The sound of those particular hard consonants made my husband want to raise his fists, but he held back. What, we asked, was that? "Funny-Looking Kid," he said nonchalantly. Seeing our incredulous expressions, he backpedaled, explaining he hadn't meant to impugn our strikingly handsome son's appearance. What he meant was that Josh was not a typical child in terms of his academic or behavioral development. But Josh was neither mentally ill, learning disabled, nor ADD. The doctor said this was good news; that our eccentric son would eventually make his talents work for him. In due time, he would get his act together. He advised us to provide Josh with a predictable daily routine and consistent discipline.

"Relax," he assured us. Given my husband's and my educational achievements, studies showed our son would make it, too.

During the next few months, my husband and I worked hard to follow his prescription, even as our son became more defiant. We encouraged his teachers to be stricter, to show him there were consequences for repeatedly leaving his books at home and tuning out stuff he found boring.

We sporadically returned to the psychologist for pep talks, as Josh grew more demoralized by his poor performance in school, which was largely a result of his inability to meet the requirements of the daily routine. Feeling sorry for him, we, for a while, resorted to hiding his report cards, so he'd forget to ask about his grades.

Yet we also convinced ourselves that things would turn out okay, because Josh was thriving in other ways. He had spent happy summers away at wilderness camp, made new friends, and by eleven had developed a sharp wit. He was such good company that a friend's parents invited him to spend a week skiing with them.

In his unique way, Josh seemed to be proving that my husband and I had been wrong.

Then, on a Monday afternoon during the first weeks of fifth grade, Josh arrived home with horrible news. He told me that, since the morning, he had been having trouble seeing, and now everything looked blurry. After giving him a hug, we headed straight to our nearby children's hospital. The next four hours were frightening and baffling. Josh kept asking me what I thought he had—a question I had no answer for, but one I was obsessed with myself. At one point, I found myself remembering that 1970s tearjerker *Death Be Not Proud*, about the boy dying of a brain tumor. Then I envisioned my son not as the architect he hoped to become, but as the blind panhandler who routinely stopped me on my way to work.

The ER doctors could not provide us with a cause for his condition, though they reassured me that there was no sign of any tumor. They recommended we see an ophthalmologist and a neurologist for a more thorough workup. The next morning, for the first time in five years, I tied Josh's shoes.

During the eye exam, Josh bungled the letter chart test. Yet, to my surprise, the doctor insisted that the rest of the examination showed normal function. With Josh standing next to me, he told me to give my son "a kick in the rear" and send him back to school. Though I walked out raging at his insensitivity and certain that this doctor must be a quack, a second ophthalmologist told us the same thing, albeit in a more professional way. But he still thought a neurological exam was needed. At the end of that hellish week, my despondent and blind son and I took the hour's drive to the brain specialist. As we got closer to our destination, Josh offered startling news. He could make out the words on the exit signs. *Hallelujah!* I felt like yelling. Maybe miracles really did happen in the Bible Belt.

Though my son had his eyesight back, the neurologist wanted to make sure all was truly well. And we needed to understand why this had happened. He concluded Josh had been a victim of hysterical blindness, a condition where the patient perceives loss of vision though the causes are purely emotional. With genuine concern, he explained that this was more common than most doctors recognized. When I discussed Josh's condition with his pediatrician, he also responded sympathetically. He added that although Josh's episode was a more dramatic reaction to stress than most, it was not that different than when a kid complains of stomachaches because of stress. And he warned that we shouldn't see this episode as "faking," because children or adults with hysterical illnesses feel symptoms—pain, blindness, or even paralysis. Though I shiver thinking back on that episode, I'm ultimately grateful for it: It was Josh's way of telling us that he needed rescuing—fast.

My husband and I immediately sprang into action and pursued a sound diagnosis of Josh's emotional health. Eventually, we received assistance from neuropsychologists who were child-development experts. After a thorough evaluation, they concluded Josh had non-verbal learning disorder (NVLD) and told us we had never heard of it because the syndrome had only been recently defined and researched. They explained that NVLD children usually speak beautifully and act like sponges with information they read or hear. But, they can be clumsy, socially awkward, and extremely disorganized. They have problems dissecting visual material and find abstract reasoning, especially math, extremely challenging. (Despite his love of architecture, Josh had always struggled in math.) This disconnect, which centers in the brain, makes these kids anxious and depressed. They surmised that Josh might also be affected by attention deficit disorder but advised us to bring him back after some months of behavior interventions before officially addressing that possibility.

When we heard this, my husband and I felt relieved that someone truly understood our child. Josh's blindness was symptomatic of his feeling that his life was spinning out of control. He knew he was bright, yet he couldn't handle the routine stuff that came naturally to others. His episode had been triggered by returning to school after a relaxing summer away. He had been just two weeks into fifth grade and had begun a new routine, consisting of a rotating schedule and multiple teachers for different subjects. Josh had barely kept up before; this was more than he could handle. On the particular day that he went blind, my husband had accompanied Josh to his first class, because he had forgotten to bring home all his work during the previous weekend, and he wanted to talk to the teacher. The anxiety about having failed to meet typical demands, plus the embarrassment of having his dad show up, sent Josh reeling.

Understanding Josh's condition has vastly improved both his life and our own. Now that we all know his difficulties are caused by brain chemistry, we get less frustrated, and he's not so hard on himself. And Josh can finally display his unique talents—his creativity, flair for public speaking, and intellectual curiosity—because we've been able to put a support system in place for him, at home and at school. He sees a behavioral psychologist who has taught him relaxation techniques and mnemonic devices for remembering everyday tasks. He now takes math tests in a quiet room without distractions. To Josh's delight, he can also use technology to his benefit: Since his written work had always been sloppy, he now types all his homework on the computer. He also uses a digital recorder to tape complex lectures, and his more cooperative teachers provide him with their PowerPoint notes. We know he's come a long way, because he's still got the electronic organizer with the alarm feature he got for Hanukkah.

SECTION 2

Taking Care of You

In 2001 I made two major life changes: I began a high-powered job at *Glamour* magazine, complete with coworkers I adored and respected. And my husband and I moved our family from the rural outer suburbs of New York City to a brownstone in Brooklyn, so that I could have a shorter commute and be closer to the city I loved. On the outside, I had it all; inside the walls of my beautiful new home, though, life was falling to pieces.

After a twelve-hour stint at the office, I'd come home to find that I was the only one with an ounce of sanity left to deal with Toby's bizarre behaviors. My husband worked at home, and by dinnertime he had already helped our babysitter put out too many family fires to have much energy for anything else. (This was before Toby was diagnosed with sensory integration dysfunction, and we were mystified by how controlling and sensitive he was.) A typical evening went something like this: Whip off work clothes, scarf down dinner—usually a few scoops of peanut butter and an apple for me, or leftovers from the kids' five o'clock dinner—build a complicated Lego structure with Toby, switch with Jeff and play American Girl dolls with Emily, cajole Toby into taking a bath, break up fight between Emily and Toby, wrestle Toby into a bear hug to keep him from spinning and crashing into the furniture during pre-bedtime tantrums, read stories, tell stories, rub Toby's back, snuggle with Emily, start doing work at my home computer until my son came upstairs to say he couldn't sleep, put Toby back in bed with warm milk, do more work, watch Toby throw up because he drank his milk too fast, clean up sheets, put Toby back in bed . . . and so on. Needless to say, when Toby finally closed his eyes for the night, I was lying catatonic beside him in his twin bed.

I figured Toby's difficult behavior had a lot to do with our move, so I began to scratch down notes in the back of my Filofax about when he had his tantrums, when he wouldn't eat, when he yelled at his sister, when he wouldn't go to bed, and when he woke up with nightmares. At first, the problem seemed contained to his hours at home. Then his preschool teacher called me at my office, saying, for the second day in a row, that my son was crying inconsolably and wouldn't talk to the school nurse—he would have to be sent home. Soon my son's behavior permeated my work life: I got daily calls from weary babysitters, my depressed husband, and my usually even-keeled daughter complaining about my son's wild tantrums and rude behavior. Some days I had emotional whiplash from switching back and forth from work to home pressures. Other days, I admit, I just didn't take calls from friends or family—I knew my assistant would let me know if there was an emergency. And other days I hired a night babysitter and stayed at the office late so I could focus on work during tough deadlines.

One particularly hellish evening when my husband was having a night out with the guys and our bedtime routine had gotten way out of hand (the three of us eventually ended up wearily curled up in my bed sobbing), I snuck off when the kids began snoring and called my dad, who has been a psychiatrist since 1972. I asked him, "Do we need help? What is wrong with my son?" My dad, not one to panic or overstate the case, calmly said he could see us unraveling. He didn't make any specific recommendations, except to say that if a group of smart adults like us couldn't figure out what was going on with Toby, then, yes, we probably needed the help of a child therapist.

The following weekend, my parents drove down from Connecticut to celebrate my daughter's birthday. My dad, witnessing Toby's erratic behaviors firsthand, said, with complete certainty this time, that if we didn't do something about the problem, we were all, including my daughter, going to be emotional wrecks. I think the official S.O.S. conversation took place on a street corner near a deli, with Jeff by my side, barely. "You can't *not* do it," my dad said in his authoritarian tone. "I don't care if you are into therapy or not, Jeff. You, Toby, and Denise— maybe even Emily—need to see a therapist. You are all under a lot of stress." He said he couldn't possibly offer a diagnosis, but he knew something in our lives needed to change.

I needed some time to think, to process everything. But with my hectic work schedule and my daughter craving my attention, too, there just wasn't a minute in the day to sit back and ponder. Life inside the whirlwind was scary and maddening. At the time, I couldn't see how truly fragile I had become. But as I read the essays in this section, I was reminded of how much coffee I drank, how much gum I nervously chewed, how much yelling I did. Sometimes when I have a bad dream, I'll remember bits and pieces of the dream throughout the day; similarly, like a nightmare, the parents who spoke so honestly and intimately in this section brought it all back for me. I saw myself for what I really was back then—a young, successful basket case.

The parents in this section have an enviable sense of self-awareness. I admire how they found ways to sustain themselves during the most trying days. I regret that I didn't have a copy of Lorena Smith's powerfully written "I Broke All the Rules Today" on some of those occasions when I was on the verge of losing it. After a horrendous morning, this mother of an autistic child takes her son for a ride in the stroller to calm both of them down, only to run into a put-together-just-so neighbor. She writes about how she feels that she has hit rock bottom, how messy her own life is, until her son stands up in his stroller and, with a poignant gesture, shows her how much he loves her. In that moment, her survival strategy became clear: Gain energy from the moments you love your child with all your heart, and don't let the low moments sap your energy. That way, there will be something left for you—of you—at day's end.

Cutting even closer to home for me was Marla Davishoff's story about her six-year-old son who struggles with anxiety and nonverbal learning disability. The sense of loving your child while at the same time simply losing it on him is captured perfectly in Davishoff's essay. When I first read it, it reminded me of a day when my boss took me out to lunch. We were waiting to be seated, making small talk, and she said, "Do you ever just think how precious your child is—how you can't wait to have another?" All I could think about was how I'd nearly wrung Toby's neck the night before because he refused to fess up to something—I can't remember what now. I had berated him. I said a few insulting things to him that I wished I could take back. I had not for one second thought of how precious he was. Of course I loved him, but sometimes I couldn't feel a thing but sheer rage. Davishoff's writing showed me the value of letting go of your frustrations—of not carrying them around with you like overstuffed luggage. I feel more alive and sane when I can get some physical and emotional distance from my son. Every day that I buy myself an hour or two without thinking about caring for him, or feeling guilty for not being with him, the more understanding I am when I return to his side.

The first time I heard a parent directly express that they nearly killed themselves because they were so depressed about life with a special-needs child was when I read Laura Cichoracki's account of life with her six-year-old autistic son. There was so much desperation in her writing that I found myself begging for her to regain some control over her depression as I read it. And she did. She begs others to understand that calling a doctor for not only your child's problems but for *your* problems is not a defeat.

All the stories in this section are life-affirming, and they prove that putting on your oxygen mask first, *then* taking care of your child's—just as they say to do on an airplane—is the best way to survive. Exercise, hobbies, chats with friends, time for therapy—none of it should be a source of guilt. If you can manage to stay whole and happy, your family will be, too.

Mother's Helpers

Dawn

Dawn is the mother of ten-year-old Jessica, who was diagnosed with Turner's syndrome, a rare chromosomal disorder that affects only girls and is often accompanied by physical symptoms and heart abnormalities. She also has high-functioning autism and early-onset bipolar disorder. She and her family live in New Jersey.

Ten years ago, I was looking down at my baby daughter in the kitchen one morning, as she sat in her bouncy seat, and her eyes were turning out in opposite directions—and I just lost it. After needing kidney surgery at two months and being told to "keep an eye on her other kidney and heart," I couldn't handle another health issue. I stood by the sink as the water ran, and I cried. I remembered seeing a scene like this on a soap opera once, before Jessica was born, and thinking, *Oh, please, this is so melodramatic. Get over it!* In the past, my response to stress had always been "take it one day at a time." Postpregnancy, though, everything seemed different. I was having trouble making it from one hour to the next—let alone making it through a whole day.

So there I was, moored to the kitchen sink in a state of panic and fear, sobbing. What did my daughter's future hold for her? For my husband? For me? I slid down onto the cold tile floor and cried so hard, and from so deep inside of me, that, to this day, I pray that I will never return to that abysmal state again.

I was staring at the phone and wanting to call my sister Sharon, who lived down the street, but for one self-conscious moment I hesitated. I didn't want anyone—not even my sister—to think I couldn't handle this nightmare. When I finally did dial her number, she, of course, came over right away. She walked with Jessica for an hour inside the house while I just sat in a kitchen chair feeling numb—and shocked. I never knew it was possible to feel so incredibly overwhelmed.

Though I'd never felt entirely in control of my life, I'd always dealt with things. I'd adapted. But this—this was just too much. How did people do it? When I was a teenager my father had been in and out of the hospital every month for two years straight at one point. My mother always bore it in stride and took care of things efficiently and lovingly. I wasn't sure I could be like her. The more I imagined what my daughter's life was going to be like—in and out of hospitals, severely handicapped, nearly blind—the more difficult it was to accept. I thought: *If I hear the phrase "God never gives you more than you can handle" one more time, I am going to scream.* Worse, I felt totally incapable of handling Jessica's needs—the needs of my own daughter. I wondered, *How am I supposed to take care of a daughter with so many special needs when I have to call someone to come over just to comfort her?*

My mom had seven children, and my five older sisters and one older brother have ten children between them. It had always been my understanding that they all did it—and I am not saying easily—without having meltdowns. But because of my own feelings that day, I began to wonder: Maybe my sisters did have low periods. They just didn't talk about them. It's possible that Mom *did* sit in her kitchen and cry for an hour about how she was going to keep her children on the right path when my older siblings were in school and the younger ones were napping. She had seven children between the ages of one and seventeen, and no car. Often my dad didn't get home until nine or ten at night. When I did ask her, some months later, she confessed that she had, in fact, found herself in the kitchen sobbing more than once.

The day Sharon came over, after allowing myself to cry and cry, I gradually began to feel a sense of relief. Once I had gotten it all out, I went outside for a while to get my breathing in order and to calm myself. When I came back inside, Sharon was calmly walking Jessica around the living room. It was then that she looked me in the eye and told me that while all of my siblings have children, none has had to deal with the kind of stress I have with a child with so many health issues. She told me they were all so proud of me, and that it was okay if I reached out and asked for help sometimes. Realizing then that my brother and sisters thought of me as someone they could respect, and not just the baby of the family, gave me the strength to move forward and acknowledge that I was dealing with exceptional circumstances.

Over the next ten years, Jessica's illness became even more complicated. To date, she has had fifteen surgeries, including surgery to correct a heart murmur, ear tubes, mouth surgery, and surgery to remove tumors in her bones. She has also been diagnosed with high-functioning autism, and doctors suspect that she may be bipolar.

And despite, or maybe because of, Jessica's diagnosis, I have found creative ways to keep the rest of my family "healthy." For the first few years, my husband, Bob, accompanied me to all of Jessica's appointments, but there were so many, and they were so frequent that he could no longer take that much time off work. Instead, he would come home from work and take care of Jessica for a few hours, so that I could decompress while I cooked dinner, without having to hold and soothe her.

I now take a more proactive approach to life: I started seeing a therapist who specializes in families with unique medical needs. He is aware of all the issues that often arise with children with medical and behavioral diagnoses. I make sure Bob and I talk on a regular basis about the things in our lives that we can be grateful for. I don't allow my emotions to build up as they did for six months, when Jes was first born. No more trying to be a supermom on the outside and feeling scared to death on the inside. I keep the lines of communication open between me and the doctors and Jes's teachers, as well as between me and Bob. Communication is the secret to my sanity. When Jes gets a new teacher, I send them a brief note about her, explaining her health issues. When I need help from Bob, instead of waiting for him to volunteer or guess what I need, I ask him.

In the year following my kitchen-sink meltdown, I also joined two mothers' groups. I split my time between them—one with so-called normal moms who did not have sick children, so I could enjoy the average things Jes might do, like library programs, birthday parties, trips to local farms; the other, a group for moms of kids involved in special-services programs, like early-intervention programs, physical therapy, occupational therapy, and speech therapy. It has been extremely therapeutic to share my experiences with moms facing similar issues.

It was, and is, often helpful for me to remind myself that even the president of the United States employs an entire staff of people to specialize in different areas of the government; he can't possibly know or do everything himself. Over time, I learned that I had to set up my own "cabinet" of sorts. I found a strong medical advocate—a pediatrician who had Jessica's best interests at heart. I sought out an education advocate in the school community whose opinion I respect and have allowed him to guide me through the maze of special services offered. My best friend meets me for a drink and dessert once a month to just laugh (and cry) with me about how crazy life can get. And my religious faith has given me the strength to make the tough decisions.

Finally, twice a year, I stay overnight at a nearby hotel for the sole purpose of grabbing some time to myself—to eat dinner by myself, sleep by myself, and eat breakfast by myself. Just to decompress, really. I don't try to fill this time with socializing or visiting; it's alone time for me to take a long bubble bath and sleep in a king-size bed with lots of pillows. While I sometimes worry that we can't afford the hundred dollars my night in the hotel will cost me, I quickly realize that we can't *not* afford it. I need to rejuvenate, or I will be of little help to my family.

When I keep the important things in perspective, everything else seems to fall into place.

Private Session in Progress

Richard Ellenson

Richard Ellenson is the father of Thomas, age eight,
who has cerebral palsy. Thomas cannot eat, speak,
or walk unassisted. The Ellensons live in New York City.

This is what our therapist told us: "Lora, you're a doctor. When you break the rules or make a mistake, people can die. But, Richard, you're in advertising. You're paid to take risks. You two chose your professions because of who you are. By nature, you will have completely different reactions to almost any situation."

Of course! That explained it all.

For the first time, I understood why Lora had dealt with our son Tom's cerebral palsy the way she had these past six years, since the day he came home from twelve days in the neonatal intensive care unit, or the NICU, as they called it. They had told us that day that Tom's health was fine. "You have a perfectly healthy baby boy," they had said—but Lora had continued to be acutely observant of him. She could let go of nothing.

She would play a game with him, asking, "How big are you getting?" then pulling Tom's arms up and out to his sides and saying, "Sooo big!" And when she did, she felt tautness in his arms, an inability to stretch, an unwillingness in his muscles. She watched him play with toys as he tilted in his standing saucer, tipping over too many times, and she worried that his hand grasped awkwardly, that he never tried to pass things from one hand to the other. When he lay on the floor on his Gymboree play mat, Tom would turn his head to look at us, but he didn't push upward with his arms or arch his back as we'd seen other kids do. Instead, his eyes twinkled, but did so from where his head lay; and his hands, as often as not, seemed most comfortable in small fists.

Six months later, it became clear that Tom had cerebral palsy. And Lora began following even more closely every manifestation of our son's condition. It was as if she thought that by observing him, she could control his fate.

Lora had charted Tom's milestones relentlessly from the day he came home from the NICU—both the milestones he made and those he didn't. She kept the charts in her nightstand drawers. She monitored his caloric intake. She constantly watched for abnormal movements, for any deviation in appetite. She made lists of what he ate.

She had Tom's physical therapists write summaries of his progress each time they visited. For two years, Lora insisted our nanny keep a journal of Tom's bowel movements.

Now, as our therapist sat in her chair and spoke to us as she had for nearly a year—measured, insightful, forming her words so she never took sides—I could see everything clearly: how the love Lora had for our son had come up against her meticulous nature, against the reflexes she had as a doctor. I suddenly saw how this had transformed her natural concerns into a maniacal accounting of fluids, movements, milestones, and measurement. How the simple joy of being a mother had been flattened by the weight of added responsibility, and how Lora had been completely disoriented by a world in which every physical law, every expectation, had changed.

Certainly, Lora was aware of Tom's spirit; she understood how he approached each day: happy, upbeat, relentlessly optimistic, focused not on experiences he might be deprived of, but on the many ones available to him, even if in an imperfect sense. And there were, of course, the many simple moments we enjoyed as a family, huddling on the sofa to read storybooks, walking aimlessly down the street to the music of idle chitchat, lying together on the floor tickling and giggling, just falling into each other's arms and catching each other's happy eyes. But despite these light moments we spent as a family, Lora's worries about Tom's physical well-being were ever present, always lingering beneath the surface. I knew that somewhere deep within her, the mother was losing out to the clinician. Her spirit was suffused with worry. Or, perhaps, maternal instinct is even more incomprehensible to a male than I imagine: Perhaps I just could not understand what it means to want to completely protect a child; to not only spiritually, but also physiologically, nurture that child.

But at that moment, sitting on our therapist's couch, I understood. It was so simple.

Lora wasn't like me: She couldn't just float weightless in our new world, giving in to a naive belief that we could just sit back and will all to be okay. She couldn't simply stumble through the sadnesses and challenges that are also born when one's child has cerebral palsy. Lora was constantly looking for tethers, safety lines that would keep her safe, rooted to all that her maternal instinct cried out for. Instead, faced with a child who was, yes, beautiful, charming, fun, and playful, but who was also in a wheelchair, nonverbal, unable to feed himself—so dependent, not in spirit, but in physical reality—Lora was looking for an intricate cat's cradle of reassurance. She desperately needed to find some sort of structure, some tenuous support where she could feel things would be all right.

In the short silence of the moment after our therapist offered her analysis, in the second or so during which all this went through my mind, I was swept up in my understanding of Lora, awash in appreciation of all she felt, of all she must consider. I looked to Lora, ready to tell her how much I loved this about her. To tell her that I understood.

But she spoke first. "Exactly," she said to our shrink. "It's why I have to do everything. Richard just wants to have fun. He's a great father. But for him, it's all about fun."

Well, of course. Fun is what makes men and sons click. Our relationships with our sons keep us going, well beyond the age when knees give out, or a middle-age gut makes those three-steps leading to a layup not only outside routine, but also outside your sphere of what seems possible.

It's true: I want to play games with Tom. Watch movies with him. Lie on the sofa amid football and potato chips. Talk men talk—boy talk with him. Talk about rock and roll, and sports, and, well, girls. Tell knock-knock jokes and make stupid faces. These things are eternal, infinite, born at the moment the X and Y chromosome meet. And I'm not going to deprive our relationship of them just because he happens to have been born with cerebral palsy.

When Tom and I hang out, fun is what you see. It's a different rhythm perhaps—it's got its quirks—but he and I, Tom and I, are hanging mano a mano, father and son. It's not that I don't take Tom's condition seriously, or recognize the importance of caring for him well and responsibly, or that I haven't spent many sleepless nights worrying about his future. I just show my concern differently than Lora. I suppose I just feel that, if you can find a way to make life fun, to make it lighter, why not do so?

My relationship with Tom is not the same as Tom's relationship with Lora. Not better, not worse, but ours to share as father and son. It's Tom's life and it's my life, and we are romping through it. Hopefully, as our family evolves together, Lora's and my understanding of our different approaches to Tom, to life, will deepen, and together, we will provide him both the care and joy every child deserves.

Only Human

Marla Davishoff

*Marla Davishoff of Deerfield, Illinois, is the mother of
Levi, a six-year-old kindergartner who struggles with
anxiety and nonverbal learning disability.*

I couldn't believe my ears. Did I actually hear her tell my five-year-old son that he scribbles like a baby? Did I see her grab his cheeks and forcefully turn his head toward his homework as she bellowed, *"Pay attention!"*? I couldn't believe that tears rolled down her cheeks faster than they rolled down his as she asked him, *"Are you stupid?"* If she were his teacher, she would be suspended. If she were his therapist, she would be sued. But she wasn't. The person degrading this special-needs child was me—his mom.

This experience with my child seems surreal. I find my conscience floating above us, observing, as my body sits at the kitchen table with my son, Levi, as we do his homework. I can't imagine who on earth this woman berating and humiliating my son is. Make her stop. Explain to her that he is not doing this on purpose. After all, aren't all children born with an innate desire to learn and adapt? When a child struggles, don't we need to find an alternative method to help him? Perhaps this woman needs to change her expectations. A child wouldn't intentionally look away from the paper when he tries to write his name or pick up a pen and hold it wrong on purpose.

As I observe more, I wonder why this woman can't be more patient and understanding with my son. Doesn't she know how much I love this child? Doesn't she know how much I have sacrificed to give him everything he needs? I don't mean sacrifice in the way parents of typ-ical children do. I mean everything: pouring myself into home-therapy programs, or fighting the school administration to get him an aid in the classroom, or turning my living room into a therapy gym. I prom-ised myself long ago that if he can't do his homework, I will certainly overcompensate and do mine.

But wait—I am this woman. It is I who am degrading my own son. Although my frustrations are usually expressed only to my close circle of family and friends, yes, sometimes I actually take them out on Levi. I know that I need to learn how to stop.

What if I pretended to be his therapist? After all, I did quit my job as a social worker to stay home and take care of him. Or maybe I need to disinvest myself from him. But how can I distance myself from my own son? Unfortunately, I don't have the answers. There was no "Parenting Your Special Needs Child 101" seminar in graduate school. Once, when I was nearing the end of my rope, I demanded, absurdly, that Levi address me as "Mrs. Davishoff," as though I were one of his teachers at school. I thought that this would encourage him to respect me and help him to concentrate more on his homework. Of course, instead, he focused on the silliness of this formal way of addressing his mother. Shortly thereafter, I also became aware that I did not want to be his teacher. I wanted to be his *mom*.

A mom is someone who is sympathetic to her child's struggles. I try to remember, for instance, that the exercises he does to strengthen his body and mind are harder on him than they are on me. It has taken some time for me to stop complaining about the stress of hav-ing my life turned upside down to care for a child with special needs. The intense therapy and tutoring schedule that we follow requires me only to chauffeur him to half a dozen appointments a week, while Levi is the one who actually participates in the intense and vigorous programs that teach him how to compensate for his disability.

As I reflect more on my out-of-body experience, I realize that I must find the strength to let go of my own frustrations. Just as Levi doesn't intentionally perform poorly at school to aggravate me, so, too, do I not want to intentionally aggravate him. Perhaps the solution is to put the homework aside for now and take a break. Let's face it, his disability is not going to change whether we complete this particular assignment or not. After all, we have been dealing with his weaknesses since his two-month checkup when his pediatrician noticed that he had missed his first milestone—smiling.

I know I need to take a moment to appreciate how hard he is trying. I need to remember that he didn't ask for this. I need to remind myself that it is harder to be a child who struggles with a disability than it is to be that child's parent.

Crash Landings

Laura Cichoracki

Laura Cichoracki is the mother of Patrick, a six-year-old son with autism. She and her family live in Osceola, Indiana.

It's a fact you learn to live with: When you are raising a child with autism, there will be times that are so unnaturally difficult as to numb your senses, so disastrous as to be comic, so heartbreaking as to crush your soul, so frustrating and so maddening and so overwhelming all at the same time that you fear you will lose your mind.

Three years ago, I snapped: I reached a depression so deep, it seemed as though I would never come out of it—but I did, and you can, too.

My first crash came about a year into my quest to make my son, Patrick, better. I had been coping with the diagnosis, which came one month shy of his third birthday. I took him to every autism specialist in our state, ran him through every medical test covered by insurance (and argued with insurance to cover still more), and got him into preschool and gymnastics and music-therapy classes for socializing. I felt confident that I could "fix" him in time, with all my dedication and hard work and love.

My depression really surfaced when Patrick was in preschool. School seemed to amplify the visible differences between him and his peers. My son had developed a nasty biting habit, which I later realized was his means of communicating pain or frustration. He had bitten me a number of times and had left horrible bruises on my body. When he bit his aide at preschool, I lost it. I picked up my son and carried him kicking and screaming like a rabid wolverine straight to the doctor's office. Turned out that he had a massive ear infection. He was back to his old self within two days, and after that, the biting pretty much stopped.

I had more difficulty recovering, though. I worried constantly about his future. I felt overwhelmed by the physical demands of caring for my child (not to mention my home). Patrick was like Looney Tunes' Tasmanian Devil—on speed. He was destructive and wild, and by the time I wrapped my head around what it would take to clean up one mess, like an entire gallon of milk spilled into the couch cushions, he was onto his next feat, like dumping a canister of flour on the floor so that he could watch the dust billow in the sunlight. His curiosity and his sensory dysfunction led him to eat hazardous objects, fall off furniture, and break things. Once he urinated into a DVD player and nearly set the house on fire. And all of this would happen while my back was turned, going to the bathroom, or trying to clean or do laundry, or, heaven forbid, answer the phone. I could never, ever, let my guard down, and by the end of the day, the strain of always trying to stay one step ahead of his overactive mind exhausted me physically and mentally.

I wasn't eating right, I wasn't showering regularly, I wasn't sleeping well. I never made time to get out of the house to do something enjoyable, because I was afraid of the catastrophe that I felt certain would be waiting for me when I returned. Reading at the local coffee house for an hour hardly seems worth it when faced with coming home and having to figure out how to clean an entire bottle of liquid dish soap out of upholstery, or clean bathroom-accident stains off the rug, or scour crayon off the walls. I was tired—all the time. I was grouchy, and my husband was tired of hearing about it, which added to my resentment toward my life. My husband is not good with the touchy-feely aspects of a relationship. His response to hearing me complain was to get defensive and withdraw, inviting me to file for divorce, which was laughable since nobody on this planet can handle the task of caring for Patrick as well as I can.

I put on a good face in public, but in the most private recesses of my being, I felt my heart start to die a little. Eventually, I started to entertain the notion that if I were dead, I could at least get a decent nap. When those morbid and nonsensical thoughts morphed into a fleeting consideration of blowing out the pilot light on the stove and sticking my head in the oven, I called my own doctor. I was prescribed Zoloft, and it was the best thing I ever did to take care of myself.

I struggled *a lot* with the decision to call my doctor. It felt tantamount to admitting defeat. I felt like I was admitting that I didn't have faith in my son's ability to grow up to be a functional member of society, and that I didn't have faith in my ability as a parent. The weeks leading up to this decision were stunningly painful. I felt as though I wasn't mother or woman or human enough to take care of business without resorting to a chemical crutch.

But the medication made room for me to function. I had more patience, more ability to handle stress. And while the bad times still came and left, I was not nearly as despondent. Patrick continued in preschool and in therapy. As he grew and learned, the tantrums got fewer, although they were still fairly shocking. But with the help of Zoloft, I stopped thinking that life was a cruel joke and was able some days to laugh, even, at the ingenious way he wreaks havoc. I no longer woke up every morning thinking, "Oh, God, what is going to go wrong today, and can I at least brush my teeth before the $#@! hits the fan." Then I unexpectedly got pregnant. I had to stop taking my medication because of the pregnancy, and then because I began nursing my daughter.

After the baby was born, when Patrick was five, he started behaving terribly again: smacking himself in the head with his fists, biting his wrists so hard that they bled (the teachers asked me if an animal had bitten him), trying to slap the baby, screaming this god-awful high-pitched whine-shriek that was like nails on a chalkboard and an ice cream headache all at the same time. I had no idea which kid to attend to and which to let scream, and how to get the house quiet again. And the dishes were not done. And the laundry was so far behind that when the school called to tell me Patrick had an accident in the bathroom and needed a change of clothes, I didn't have a clean pair of jeans ready. And I started working again, doing medical transcription at home, part-time—the hours were flexible, expenses minimal. The money? Spent before I cashed the check.

All of these things kept piling up on me like layers of blankets, eventually threatening to suffocate me. Frustration quickly led to being overwhelmed, and that led to being angry and resentful all over again. And that led to nasty, mean, irrational thinking. Like how I hated being a mom, and I hated my kids, and I hated my life during afternoons when the kids were screaming and dinner was burning and the phone was ringing and the dryer had just broken and the laundry was stacked up. I was so tired during that period, I perpetually felt like puking, but my husband was at work, and I knew I'd have to work later that night, so I couldn't even dream of getting some rest. There was nobody close by to call for help, and even if there were, my house was such a mess that I couldn't possibly have let anybody in or they might have called Child Protective Services or maybe the health department—which would remind me that I hadn't showered in eight days and my son just had pooped on the floor.

So I snapped. Big time. Finally, one afternoon, my body let off steam in a primal way, because I was no longer in the realm of civilized society. I screamed with so much gusto that I actually wet my pants. I pounded my fists on the cabinets because I needed to share my pain, but I can't—and won't—direct it at my children. I cried. I prayed. And I turned around to see that my kids had seen this whole giant tantrum, and they were frightened and crying. They wanted me to comfort them but didn't want to be near me. I hated myself for setting such a bad example for them. I hated myself for being the one to put that look on their faces. I hated myself for hating my life. I felt like I had disappointed everybody who counted on me.

I got depressed all over again. I sank to my knees on my filthy kitchen floor and sobbed uncontrollably. And I prayed again.

Thankfully, the last round of deep depression lasted only a few weeks. I was fortunate to be surrounded by other moms who understood my pain, women I had met through Patrick's school and therapy who could be supportive and empathic, as well as family members who couldn't really understand, but were patient and comforting and nonjudgmental nonetheless. One might think from reading this that my husband is ignorant, or insensitive, or a real jerk. Yet, in reality, he is my rock. We take turns dealing with our emotions and working to buoy the spirits of the other. We approach life in different ways. I tend to take a "Just cry it out, honey, it will be all right" approach, whereas my husband prefers more of a "Buck it up" approach. My husband is the guy who refuses to cry at funerals. When I am depressed, it's hard to focus on what he means and not what he says. But sometimes, having somebody remind me that it could be much worse, and that I have met mothers of other children with disabilities *way* more severe than the ones my son has, is a blessing. When I am at my weakest, my husband gives me the strength I need to get a grip.

If I've learned anything from what I've been through, it's that I never want to put that look on the faces of my beloved babies ever again. If this means using medication again to calm my son (or myself) during his periods of frustration and self-injurious behavior, so be it.

My son will be six in a few months, and he is still nonverbal. We are learning to use an augmentative communication device, a device that allows Patrick to press icons to compile sentences to tell us what he wants or needs or thinks. He can't talk, but he has shown us that he is able to read and spell at approximately a second-grade level. He is currently mainstreamed into a very large kindergarten class at the local public school—he and a boy with Down's syndrome are the only special-needs children. With the assistance of an aide, he is doing well. When we're out in the world together, Patrick still has trouble with sensory overload, and he gets overstimulated a lot. I often get looks and whispers from onlookers in stores and restaurants. Occasionally, an elderly lady will decide that I need a lecture from her on what "good mommies" do, and what is needed to make a "brat" behave in public. Now, instead of cringing inside, I explain the situation. I have found that people are interested and want to know more about autism. Often they are apologetic. I now have the gumption to teach people not to judge a book by its cover.

Although there have been times over the past few years when I've felt completely isolated in what I'm going through, I know that, actually, my situation is all too common. I want other moms and dads to know that having periods of depression and anxiety does not make you inept or worthless. Feeling that death might be preferable to spending one more torturous second in this insane period of your life does not make you a weak person. It makes you an over-whelmed person who needs support. This might mean a shoulder to cry on, or a support group, or a trip to your doctor. You have to find what fits. Needing help comes with the territory when you care for an autistic child: *Accepting* help—however difficult that might be, be-cause of what it implies to you—is imperative. And when you do have those overwhelming feelings, remember that you are not alone.

Danger: Do Not Compare Child to Others

Anonymous

Written by an East Coast mother of a three-year-old boy who has cerebral palsy.

When my son, M, was born and doctors discovered he had brain damage, they told me he could have cerebral palsy and mental retardation, and that he might never walk or talk. After two weeks in the pediatric ICU, he came home, and I began watching him for the tiniest sign that anything was wrong—nothing escaped my eagle eye. (Was he staring blankly into space or just mesmerized by the ceiling light?) I couldn't call a doctor with every single *Is he not normal?* worry, so, instead, I began comparing M to other babies. *Uh-oh:* Other Baby at the restaurant is able to hold a rattle and shake it; M can't. *Uh-oh:* Other Baby at the mall is making cute cooing sounds; M isn't. *Uh-oh:* Other Baby at the park is able to point to what he wants; not M. The comparisons ran like ticker tape through my head, mercilessly unstoppable.

I've always been a detail-obsessed person. It's why I'm the one who pays the bills in my marriage. It's why, as I gazed at our freshly painted porch the other day, I instantly found the spot the painter smudged. Being detail oriented is something you might want to mention on your résumé, but it is a nightmare when you have a challenged child. You not only notice everything, you can't *stop* yourself from looking. At night, I'd thumb through *What to Expect the First Year*, reading the same chapters repeatedly in disbelief that M was failing to do what he should have been doing at his age. Every week, when I got the Babycenter.com update on the milestones my child ought to be reaching, I read them hungrily, grateful if M was behaving in any way close to the way he was "supposed" to. Typically, the e-mails left me heaving with sobs—big, fat tears dripping onto my keyboard.

It didn't help that trading baby accomplishments is the currency of motherhood. *"Is M walking yet?"* a colleague asked me one day, completely unaware of how devastating her question was; she'd had her baby around the same time I had M. To keep my composure, I learned to respond brightly and briefly to these queries: *"Nope! Not yet!"* became my standard reply.

Birthday parties were especially painful. Every occasion offered up a whole roomful of kids to compare M to at once, a batch of case studies. The stretch of first-year parties was truly a nightmare. At twelve months, M was barely able to sit up, couldn't feed himself or hold a bottle (the brain damage had left his arms stiff and spastic), and made no sounds. I usually sat out these events in a living room corner, holding M tight as I observed what the other kids were up to: toddling or crawling at a rapid clip, babbling, shoving cookies into their little mouths. I'd leave every party frustrated, upset, and angry at the world.

Comparing M to normally developing children was one kind of torture I invented for myself; comparing him to other challenged kids I'd see at the physical therapy center was another. Would we someday be pushing M in a wheelchair like the teenage boy with the floppy legs that I saw being wheeled down the hall? Would M drool constantly like that little girl who'd had the appointment after us? Would M not be able to respond to his name? The comparisons grew more and more irrational. One Saturday, at a sandwich shop with my husband, I watched intently as a mentally retarded man put together the turkey sandwich I'd ordered. Is this, I wondered, what M is destined for in life? Would M be able to hold down a job or live on his own? The thing is, even doctors didn't know what the future held for M; it was too early to tell. And that's what made life so damn hard.

I usually kept my compare-athons to myself. My husband, dealing with grief in his own way—namely, denial—didn't want to hear how M might be different from other kids. I didn't voice concerns around my parents, either; they're elderly, and I hesitated to add my worries to their lives. I did question friends about what their kids were doing, but not too often; I didn't want them to think I was jealous of their "normal" kids, even though I sometimes secretly was.

As M grew older, it became more and more obvious that he wasn't like other kids. At two, he went to a local music class every week with his babysitter, and once I took him on a day off from work. As the other kids jangled bells and pranced around, I tried not to lose heart over the fact that M was just crawling and still couldn't hold a drumstick. Keeping my chin up wasn't easy: Not one of the other mothers in the class said hello to me that day. Mostly, they averted their eyes. Was it because M was different from their kids? Defective? I felt so alone.

Then I had another baby—a completely healthy baby who hit all of the Babycenter.com milestones on time. One Sunday morning as our family lay in bed together—my daughter, eight months old, and M, almost three—I watched as she waved a rattle, then winced as M struggled to grasp a small ball. My husband noticed my expression and said, softly, "Honey, *stop*."

I knew I had to. The truth was that M would do things at his pace and in his own way. Comparing him to other children only made me severely anxious about his future, and did M zero good. Plus, I was spending so much time observing other kids that I wasn't fully enjoying M: his beautiful grin. His perseverance to keep at a task, no matter how hard it was for him. The way he'd stare so intensely when I read his favorite book, *The Wheels on the Bus*, and his adorable fascination with peekaboo. Focusing on what he wasn't able to do only diminished all that there was to love about M.

M is three years old as I write this. He's just as smiley as ever. He makes sounds and knows several hand signs. He listens and understands when we ask him if he'd like to go outside to play or sit down to read a book. He loves to kiss his little sister. And although he has cerebral palsy, he's *walking*.

I still dread birthday parties, but I can distract myself by helping him do activities or spooning cake into his mouth. Sometimes I still compare M to other kids. Yet when I'm at his special-needs school, I find myself making new kinds of observations: M can walk without braces; Other Child can't. M can do high-fives; Other Child can't. This isn't a mean-spirited comparison: I am just in awe of how far he's come. Ultimately, though, celebrating M's accomplishments is the best therapy for me. There's nothing like giving him a big hug. The reality of his warm, happy little body yanks my mind back to the child in front of my eyes, not the child I hope he'll be.

It Is Okay to Be Angry

Susan Marrash-Minnerly

Susan Marrash-Minnerly is an associate professor of theater at West Virginia State University and the mother of Nathan, a ten-year-old third-grader who has autism. She and her family live in Charleston, West Virginia.

It is okay—in fact, it is perfectly normal—to be angry that your child has autism. For me, dealing with my son's problems has been a long journey: Sometimes the road has been straight and smooth; sometimes there have been deep valleys of despair; and other times, there have been mountaintops of joy so high that they have rocked my world.

I vividly remember the day the journey started: I was seated in the pediatrician's office with my husband. The doctor told us that, yes, some of Nathan's developmental delays and behavior issues were probably due to his having spent the first three and a half years of his life in a Romanian orphanage. But he was worried: Despite speech and occupational therapy, Nathan wasn't really improving. He said, "I just want to be sure we are doing everything we can to help Nathan. I'd like for you to take him to a psychologist for an evaluation." *Reasonable idea*, I thought.

Soon after, we spent a long day of testing at a psychologist's office. A graduate student had been dispatched to discuss the results and observations of the testing with us. In the middle of her speech, I remember her saying, "Oh, yeah, we noticed the autism, too"—and just as nonchalantly as if she were reading off a grocery list, she began to talk about something else.

What?! Autism? Had we heard her correctly? Did she really say that?

I felt as though I had been eviscerated. I knew nothing about autism. I had visions of Nathan living an isolated, miserable life. I remember very little else about that day—except that my husband got mad and I cried. Then we left the office with our son and went shopping. That's right—shopping.

Having already planned to buy a little pool for the backyard, we went out and bought the biggest pool we could find. Nathan couldn't wait to get into the water. It was a cool day, so we set the pool up and emptied the hot-water heater twice to fill it. We sat on our back porch watching a joyful little boy frolic in his new pool—and we wept. I felt as alone as I had ever felt in my life. I could see my husband felt the same way, and as we sat there in the sunshine we grieved as though someone had died.

Over the last five years we have been through the classic stages of grief. At first we denied it. We knew the diagnosis was wrong. The graduate student must have administered the tests incorrectly. We took Nathan to other doctors, to autism specialists around the country. The diagnosis was correct.

Then we were scared. We didn't know what to do or where to turn. The graduate student had been unable to answer any of our questions about autism or about the quality of life we might expect for Nathan. She handed us a sheet of paper with a few clinics and therapists listed and said, "Go get some help, then come back in a year." That's it.

Then we felt guilty. We should have known sooner. We should have done more. We were (and sometimes still are) very angry. It was so unfair. What had this innocent child done to deserve this? Why had his whole life been taken from him? There was also a good deal of self-pity involved. *Why couldn't we just have a "normal kid?"* It wasn't fair.

It took months before our grief transformed itself into acceptance and hope. It took even longer to realize that Nathan didn't change because of the diagnosis. "Autism" was just a label. It has been five years since we first heard the words "autism" or "special needs" associated with my son. When I look back, I want to tell other parents that a child's future is worth grieving over—but it is not the end of the world.

Society indoctrinates us to accept such a narrow definition of "success"—going to an Ivy League college, making lots of money, being powerful and influential. Let me tell you what we now wholeheartedly and proudly call "success": Our son can and will look people in the eye and say hi to them. Our son can write his name. He can dress himself. Our son is verbal enough to tell us why, when he was about five years old and despite the consequence of losing a favorite activity for the day, he threw Jell-O all over the car. He grins from ear to ear and says, "Was funny." Our son with autism has a sense of humor! He came home from school and told us a knock-knock joke: "Knock knock," "Who's there?" which is where his joke ends, but he thinks it's incredibly funny. Nathan works so hard to achieve things that are second nature for most of us, and his every accomplishment is a cause for celebration. But in those moments of happiness, we often forget that Nathan still has, and most likely always will have, autism.

Without doubt, dealing with mental illness is a lifelong journey, and it can be a very difficult one. Nathan doesn't know that we are sometimes angry at the autism or that we sometimes cry. What he does know is that we love him, are so incredibly proud of him, and we are always here to, as he would say, "take care [him]."

I Broke All the Rules Today

Lorena Smith

*Lorena Smith is the mother of three-year-old J.J.,
who has autism. They live in Dallas, Texas.*

I broke all the rules today: The "Be Consistent" rule. The "Never Give In" rule. And especially the "Always Be Patient" rule.

I'm tired this morning. I am bone-weary. I always wondered what people meant when they said that, but I can actually feel my bones ache today.

Be patient, be consistent. Don't give in. Make him say the words. Be patient.

I haven't slept in two days. My eyes feel like they are on fire trying to keep open.

J.J. cried all night; he's still crying. I have gone over every part of his body to see if there is a bruise, a mark, an ache.

I can find nothing wrong. The cries come from the confused aching inside of him, when his world does not make sense.

Don't get angry, be patient. Be patient. Never give in, never give up.

He's still crying as I try to give my daughter breakfast. His screams echo in my head until I can't hear anything else. My hips and back feel like they are going to break because I have been walking and carrying and rocking him all night trying to comfort him from an invisible pain. I don't know what is causing it, and he can't tell me.

Who the hell made these rules up? Who wrote "Teaching Autistic Children Language"? Did Dr. Blah Blah Blah actually ever even meet an autistic child before he wrote a book about teaching them anything?

Be patient my ass.

The refrigerator door has been open all night. There is dirty laundry overflowing into the kitchen. There are no clean towels.

He flails out with his little arms and knocks over my coffee cup. Another puddle to join the puddles and stains already under my table. I can't find where the coffee spilled, though. There is cereal tracked all over the living room. He must have found where I hide the cereal boxes.

He reaches out for the gallon of milk on the table, and I try to make him say the word or make the sign. *Follow the rules, and you'll have a healthy child. He will learn language as long as you are consistent. Be patient. Be consistent.*

He is screaming too loudly to say the word, and I break the "Be Consistent" rule and hand him the milk. Anything for a minute of peace and quiet.

I decide to take him out for a walk in the stroller. Maybe he'll fall asleep.

(Maybe I'll die.)

The outdoors cheer him a little, but he still whimpers. There is an early frost on the ground, and I can hear the cows waking up and mooing at the neighboring farm.

My daughter skips ahead of us on the road, talking to the cows and the leaves on the trees. She wears one of my sweaters because I can't find any of hers. *Be patient. Breathe. Breathe.* I feel my heart rate start to stabilize.

I hear a car drive by and automatically call for my daughter to move to the side of the road. The car slows down beside me.

"Darling! Are you up exercising so early? Really you are too good! How *do* you cope? I just couldn't do it. Well, got to fly! Have a great day. Call me for coffee sometime. Bye!"

It is an acquaintance from church. *How do I cope?* Is this considered coping? What the hell does she know, anyway? I curse her to the pit of hell. I curse her perfect makeup and her perfect children. I bet her living room is immaculate and her son doesn't step on eggs and then walk through the whole house.

I bet she has no puddles on her floor.

I don't think I can stand this one more day.

I feel tears on my face.

Then I feel something else.

My precious son is standing up in the stroller, his hands on my face.

He is licking the tears from my cheeks.

SECTION 3

The Roller Coaster

Toby is seven now, and some of my most deeply satisfying moments these days are when he and I seem to have swapped roles: He assures *me* he will be okay if there is noise at a party, or if someone doesn't like him because he is "weird." I am filled with pride, seeing him laugh on a crowded playground, or use his hyperperceptiveness to discuss how he sees poverty on the street, or worries that Israel will never be safe. These are the "high times"—the ones when I am actually *thankful* for having a not-so-normal kid. My husband agrees: Helping him grow up has made us all stronger, prouder, and wiser than we might have been without him.

Still, I wouldn't wish Toby's "low lows"—his occasional uncontrollable rages, his oversensitivities, and his gnawing self-doubt—on any human being. Toby has truly taken his hits. No doubt my daughter has suffered, too. Sure, we've tried to ensure that her brother isn't consuming more than his share of emotional space in our family—but sometimes he's a force that can't be stopped.

Then again, for all the hellishness, I strongly believe that a sizable chunk of Emily's self-confidence comes from learning to thrive in a dysfunctional family. She's a masterful organizer, playdate hostess, and chief calmer-downer to little cousins. Surrounded by a crowd of family or friends, she leaps into the action playing happily amid the chaos. And despite all his issues, Toby has won Emily's heart with his incredible humor—their closeness as they giggle at a movie or as he imitates the cranky newspaper seller on our corner sends me swooning.

One thing's for sure: It has taken us a *looong* time to get to this happy, rational place. Jeff and I had several experiences getting off the wrong exit on the mental health highway before finally receiving a sound diagnosis and treatment plan for Toby. Knowing that Toby's issues would not improve without professional intervention, I made finding a therapist for us a priority; to say the least, I was disappointed by what I found in the way of help. First, there was the couples' therapist—referred to us by the psychologist on staff at Toby's preschool in Brooklyn—who ushered my husband and me into her office five minutes late, spent twenty minutes talking about how crappy insurance policies are these days, and then, in the remaining minutes, asked for the ten-cent tour of our family. Her conclusion: "From what you're telling me about your son, there's not that much that's unusual about him." She ended the hour by saying, "It sounds as though you and your husband are having difficulty agreeing on a way to discipline a stubborn child, and that the two of *you* are having problems." Thanks for the input.

Next up, Therapist Number 2. We didn't quite connect with this woman, either (also referred to us by Toby's school). We equally disliked Number 2's tone, her long-winded prattle, and her silly office doodads—at least Jeff and I had a laugh over how we agreed on something! Over the first dinner out that we'd treated ourselves to in months, we decided not to return to the counselor we now refer to as "The Woman Who Mistook Us for an Average Couple." On the upside, this gave us time to discuss the one good message she had for us (which, come to think of it, wasn't wholly different from Therapist Number 1's): You need to reign in *your* behavior—and respect each other's feelings—if your son is going to change, whatever the heck is wrong with him. We agreed that our frequent battles made him feel anxious, ungrounded, and confused about how to behave. I'm sure his big ears caught wind of our arguments over whether he could sleep in our bed, when he should be given a time-out, what to do when a "reward" chart we had set up didn't work. And I know he saw us disagree over whether he should switch schools.

Agreeing at dinner was one thing—agreeing when we were under fire was ten times harder. In the weeks following our appointment with Therapist Number 2, there were days when I listened to Toby screaming at Jeff, and Jeff screaming at Toby, and Emily crying, and I put my head down on my desk upstairs and swore. There was a day when Toby's teacher called to say he told her that he hates arguing, and that his mom and dad argue a lot—and then I was the one who sunk to a sad, frustrated place. Then there were happy days: Toby learned to ride his bike or made a new friend or slept a full night in his own bed or gave the Grandma he kicked and screamed at the last time he saw her a huge bear hug. Up and down, up and down—the emotional roller coaster sped on.

My therapist-calling binge lasted only a few weeks—maybe two months at most. Eventually, we found one excellent therapist for Toby, another for Jeff and me. But the whiplash of being a special-needs mom seemed permanent. The initial "not knowing" what was wrong with my son, and then the relief of thinking we had a diagnosis, and then again, the "not knowing" resurfacing when he did not respond well to a particular medication or therapy—combined with all of the other highs and lows my family experienced along the way—was the basis for my wanting to include this section on "The Roller Coaster."

The parents in this section haven't had the luxury, as many parents of average kids do, of a straight shot from toddlerhood to tweens. Emotionally speaking, they've gotten bounced around, kicked in the butt, sent reeling, and thrown to the ground more than a few times.

Sometimes the head-trip started just days after a child entered the world. Several of the mothers I spoke with in writing this book said that they felt as though they had been given the wrong baby in the hospital—this cranky, sickly child they held couldn't possibly be theirs. I admired the courage these mothers had that gave them the strength to tell me, a stranger, about those feelings.

But the pain of having a not-so-healthy child is not the exclusive birthright of biological mothers—adoptive parents feel quite the same pain, explains Barbara Nelson from Des Moines, Iowa, in "The Meaning of Family." When she and her husband adopted a second child, the first few months were a dream. Then, "overnight, all that changed— I still don't know why." Her son has attention deficit hyperactivity disorder (ADHD), oppositional defiant disorder (ODD), and reactive attachment disorder, the last one a common behavioral problem of children who spend time in foster care. After months of aggressive behavior, she and her husband were forced to decide whether they would follow through with adding child number five to their tribe. She remembers, "Nothing that was happening fit into my picture of what I knew about being a family."

In the last contribution in this section, Connecticut mother Lisa Lori deals with the ways in which her own autoimmune disease has affected her sons, all of whom were born with a variety of physical challenges. "Three children born under these circumstances could crush anyone, and it tested us for sure," she says. Her latest hope: A famous doctor who was recommended by the National Institutes of Health agreed to take on her medical case, to help her understand why her disease affected her children so severely when her first doctors said that was nearly impossible. The road ahead, she admits, will be a long one.

Reading this section, I felt honored to know such brave parents. I hope their stories will serve to prop you up when you get that knocked-the-wind-out-of-you feeling.

Anticipating Difference

David McDonough

David McDonough is a stay-at-home dad who lives in Titusville, New Jersey. His son was diagnosed with Asperger's syndrome at age four and a half.

Most people are skeptical when I say that I knew something was "off" the moment my son emerged from the birth canal. He was red-faced and crying, of course—nothing unusual about that. But there was real anger in that cry. It wasn't until years later that this feeling made sense. My son has Asperger's syndrome, and Asperger kids hate change. You can't give them nine months in a warm, nurturing environment and then tell them one day that the party is suddenly over. The transition is just too great.

That cry continued to obsess me over the next year. It wasn't that Jamie wailed more than other babies. It wasn't that he was completely inconsolable. It was the frustration I heard in his voice, the sense that there was something he needed that couldn't be filled with food, sleep, or love. There was always the feeling that we were missing something. What did he want? What was he trying to tell us? Were we giving him too much, or not enough, of something—attention, discipline, medicine?

For the first few years, my wife, Andrea, and I tried to tell each other that everything was normal. After all, Jamie was bright and imaginative. He walked at ten months (although he never crawled) and talked reasonably well at a year. He was cuddly and loved music. So what if he got incredibly upset at changes in schedule? What did it really matter that he had a hard time controlling his impulse to hit, pull hair, and scratch when he didn't get his way? Was it really so strange that he ran from one end of the house to the other in a determinedly repetitive pattern, as if he were comfortable only when the path was familiar, running as if his whole being depended on it? He was "only" eighteen months, and then "only" two years, and then, as a child psychologist told us, "Sounds like a typical three-year-old to me." But he wasn't. Typical three-year-olds don't grab other three-year-olds by the neck in a desperate attempt to make them stop making noise. Typical four-year-olds don't ask everyone they know (including waitresses and people on the street) for their middle names, and commit all those names to memory. Typical preschoolers are beginning to learn empathy, and to play together, as opposed to alongside one another. My son was not behaving typically. And we knew it. His preschool teacher warned us several times that he was out of control in class. He couldn't sit still at story time, couldn't keep his hands to himself, couldn't leave a subject alone when it was exhausted, and laughed (out of sheer nervousness, we found out later) when another child got hurt.

We told each other that we needed to crack down. We tried giving him more time-outs. We tried a rewards-for-good-behavior system. Nothing worked. Some of our family members thought he just needed a good spanking, but neither of us believed in that. We fretted then that some of his relatives didn't even seem to like him. We worried, of course, that we were bad parents. And, although we were trying to stay on the same page, we grew short-tempered with each other. From the time he was one until he was five, Jamie slept only until about five o'clock—and was determined that if he didn't sleep, nobody would. Worry, frustration, and lack of sleep are surefire ways to drive even the most devoted couple apart.

It is difficult to diagnose a very young child, so Jamie was about four when we finally got a definitive answer from a doctor: ADD/ADHD. We thought that solved the puzzle. Then, when our son was four and half, his new psychologist first uttered the words "Asperger's syndrome." That was a terrible moment for us. We didn't know much about Asperger's, and when a doctor, as delicately as possible, says, "It's on the autism spectrum," let me tell you, the parents are stunned. There is no word in behavioral development that is more red flag, more devastating to hear, than "autism" when mentioned in connection with your child. Besides, she had to be wrong. Don't autistic children withdraw and bang their heads against a wall? Aren't most autistic children mentally slow? That's what we had read and seen. Jamie was bright and outgoing, if clueless, socially. This warranted looking into.

So we read as much as we could on the subject. We read *Asperger's Syndrome: A Guide for Parents and Professionals*, by Tony Attwood, a leading specialist in the field, and *Pretending to Be Normal*, by Liane Holliday Willey, an educator who has Asperger's. And we explored the Web site run by the group Oasis (Online Asperger Syndrome Information and Support), which has an incredible amount of useful data, and is a great way to talk to other parents via electronic bulletin board. Hearing the stories these parents told about their children, stories that struck a familiar chord, helped convince us that our son's behavior did, indeed, fit the diagnosis he'd been given. Maybe because all along I knew there was something "different" about Jamie, the news sunk in rapidly, and after two weeks of reading and researching on our own, we acknowledged that the diagnosis (subsequently confirmed by a neurologist and a psychiatrist) was correct. "Mild Asperger's" was the official diagnosis, but when it's your child, nothing is "mild."

I have come to believe that when your child is saddled with a disability, you need to go through all the stages of grief—mourning for what might have been, and saddened by some of the limitations that are in store. It is perfectly acceptable to go through denial, rage, bargaining, and the other recognized stages before you recognize the situation for what it really is, and then begin to take pride in and enjoy your child's successes.

Dark Times Can Be
Followed by Deep Joy

Maryrose Sylvester

Maryrose Sylvester is the mother of Julianna, a three-year-old born with profound hearing loss. She and her family live in Charlottesville, Virginia.

My first words to Julianna, moments after she was born, were "I love you—and I will always protect you." To this day, I do not know what made me say them. (To our second daughter I said, simply, "I will always love you.") But for some reason—despite the fact that she was given a clean bill of health at the hospital—I had a nagging feeling that Julianna would have a tougher road ahead than we would have hoped for our little angel.

We brought Julianna home three days after she was born, cherishing our new little girl and all the happiness she brought to our family. As a new mother, I watched her milestones closely. She was our firstborn, and I worried about her eating habits, her sleep, her motor skills—everything a new mother could worry about—usually for no reason. Then, at about four months, I remember wondering if Julianna could hear. I was always unsure whether voices and music soothed her, and she did not seem to respond to doorbells or other loud sounds. It often seemed like she tuned out the noise and chaos going on around her. But I knew that when I walked into the room and called her name, she would often be comforted. Looking back, I think she sensed my presence but did not hear me. I was too afraid to push the issue further at the time.

When Julianna was four months old, her eleven-month-old cousin had his hearing retested. Shortly beforehand, his parents had noticed a sudden change in his hearing, for no apparent reason. At twelve months old, he was diagnosed with profound hearing impairment. No one knew the cause. With absolutely no family history, doctors suspected it was the result of a virus or complication in the pregnancy. Our hearts broke for him as the family rallied around him and his parents.

Little did we know, this diagnosis was only the beginning of what would become a life-altering journey for Julianna, Michael, and me.

As time went by, my worries about Julianna's hearing intensified. I caught myself secretly trying to gauge it every time we were alone together. I began banging doors, running the vacuum cleaner, running water, singing, and anything else I think of to see if Julianna would respond. But I always did it when we were alone, so that I could determine if there was a problem, without having to talk about it out loud. (I later learned that Mike was doing the same thing.) At Julianna's nine-month checkup, I asked her pediatrician about it. At first she thought her hearing seemed fine, since Julianna seemed to respond to her cues quite well. Then I told her about Julianna's cousin's recent diagnosis, and she suggested I take Julianna in for a full hearing screen. In the meantime, our sister- and brother-in-law moved quickly with their son and made the decision to pursue a cochlear implant for him. (The cochlear implant is an internally implanted device that connects to a body-worn computer processor. It has a very high success rate and can actually allow a deaf person to hear. The National Institutes of Health found it safe for use in children and adults in the mid-1990s.)

When Julianna had her full hearing screening, at nine months old, she was diagnosed with mild to moderate hearing loss in both ears. We were advised to get her hearing aids as soon as possible and to see what kind of progress she made. Trying to get a one-year-old to wear hearing aids in both ears and to keep them in—and then trying to determine if she's actually *hearing* anything with them on—was like wrestling an octopus. I'm not sure who spent more time crying in frustration—Julianna or me. After a month of struggling, Mike and I doubted that she was hearing anything more through the use of the aids.

When we took her for her hearing tests, she was less responsive than she had been just four weeks before. We pushed for a more precise diagnosis.

More tests; worse news: We were told Julianna had severe to profound hearing loss in both ears. I literally banged my head against a wall when the doctor delivered the news. This was *not* the life I wanted for my daughter. I did not want her to have to face these kinds of obstacles. The news produced fear and panic that ironically left us nearly silent for the next couple of weeks; we could barely talk to each other about what we knew. We quietly reached out to family and just held one another.

When our period of mourning had run its course, we moved into mission mode. And we found out that we were pregnant again.

I was energized and ready for the next step for Julianna: a cochlear implant. We started talking to surgeons and therapists. In the meantime, Julianna began auditory verbal therapy. Through our sister-in-law, we found a wonderful therapist. Dr. Don Goldberg immediately made us feel comfortable, and he loved Julianna, who in turn worshipped him. (To this day, she lights up when she sees him.) It was amazing to watch this one-year-old little girl sit still for an hour straight each week and "play along" with Dr. Goldberg.

As plans for Julianna's implant progressed, I was continually impressed with the top-notch care we received. And every time we drove the three hours to the University of Michigan hospital (a top pediatric cochlear implant center, where the implantation was to take place), I was reminded that it really does take a village. Julianna's hearing-rehabilitation plan included an implant surgeon, an audiologist who did the mapping of the software, an auditory verbal speech therapist, and a program coordinator.

Julianna was "implanted," as they say in the hospital, on December 1, 2003. It was a bittersweet experience. We dreaded the fact that Julianna had to have the operation but had so much hope for what it could bring to her.

Only a few hours after surgery, Julianna felt well enough to enjoy being pushed around the halls of the hospital in her stroller. We brought her home the next day.

After she was implanted, all of these people worked together to make sure my child's "map" was aligned precisely for her needs. I learned that this was not only a science, but also an art—one that takes a lot of skill and observation. Julianna's rehab team in Michigan would adjust her software and follow her verbal and visual responses to audio cues. They would try different settings and see how she responded. Each mapping session was followed by a listening exam in a sound booth to determine at what levels Julianna was beginning to consistently respond. But the real tests were done in her everyday environment. We were taught what to look for and what to pay attention to: Was Julianna able to hear from various distances, could she hear well in a noisy room, could she filter relevant from irrelevant sounds, could she hear dogs barking, birds singing, airplanes flying? We had to pay attention to everything in order to help her maximize the benefit of this new device.

Julianna's little sister, Gabriella, was born on January 8, 2004— only seven weeks after my daughter's surgery. Julianna was ecstatic to meet her new sibling. A few days later, Mike and my mom made the drive back to Ann Arbor to have Julianna's implant activated. I couldn't make the trip because of Gabriella's young age, but, luckily, the activation was videotaped. It is utterly amazing to watch. I wrote a letter to Julianna for Mike to read when they turned on her implant. I wanted her to always know how proud I was of her and how strong I knew she was—and that we would always be by her side. When the audiologist turns the implant on, Julianna drops her head in her hands and holds it there for at least five minutes. At that moment, you see her hearing real sound, probably for the first time. It is a sight that we will never forget. The initial turn-on process was a two-day event, during which Mike was taught how to use the equipment and her "map" was set. I could not wait for them to get home, so I could see her for myself.

Julianna did a great job adjusting to her new equipment and operating in the hearing world. The months to come were full of verbal stimulation—animal noises, songs, musical toys, bubble blowing, screaming. Anything we could do to encourage her to learn to listen and to pay attention to her environment. She had formal therapy two to three days per week, and we did therapy with her at home for at least an hour every day. Now, just two years after her implant, she is testing at typical levels for receptive language and near typical for expressive. It is the everyday events that have astounded me over these last few years: Julianna's Nana teaching her to say "flower" after she helped her to pick flowers for her mommy; seeing how she loves listening to her Papo's deep voice and singing with him; handing her the phone so her aunts and uncles can talk to her.

It has been a tougher journey for Julianna than any parent would like to see their child endure, but she is an amazing child. She is happy and sweet and smart and funny and busy. She will celebrate her fourth birthday in a few weeks and has just completed her first year of preschool. We are so proud of her.

The Meaning of Family

Barbara Nelson

Barbara Nelson is the adoptive mother of James,* who is seventeen and has been diagnosed with ADHD, ODD, and reactive attachment disorder. She and her family live in Iowa.

For years, we were what anyone would call an average American family. Life was just as I had imagined: mom and dad, two kids (a boy and a girl), a dog, and two cats living in a neighborhood with big trees, a big yard, and church on Sunday. My husband, John, and I had always talked about having a big family, but time just seemed to slip by, and we didn't have more kids after our daughter and son were born. Then when Manda and Bobby were six and eight, we heard about a program in our local newspaper to promote adoption of older foster care children.

My husband and I decided not to do foster care before adopting—we did not believe it was right to "try out" a child before making the decision to adopt. (We didn't have this option with our birth children, we reasoned, so why should we with our adopted children?) So we prayed, asking God to make it clear which child we were to adopt into our family. We looked at pictures of children that needed a family, and a little blonde girl named LeAnn with big brown eyes grabbed our attention. We prayed specifically for her and asked God to give her the right family.

Adopting a child can be a bumpy road—you feel like you have

---

*Names have been changed.

no control over the process. Initially, the adoption committee turned us down. They thought LeAnn would do better in a family as an only child. I had just begun to accept the fact that she would not be ours when we got a telephone call. The family they originally had in mind for LeAnn had chosen another little girl.

LeAnn officially joined our family when she was nine. At first, our new daughter had many emotional and behavioral issues. She had been in foster care since the age of two. She had been neglected by her birth parents and suffered abuse in one of the foster families. She had countless phobias. A rain cloud would send her into hysteria. Adjusting to her new school and day-care center were very difficult. If anyone came too close to her, she would hiss like a scared animal. Because of her social awkwardness, the other children at school made fun of her and called her "LeAnimal." It was heartbreaking. It was difficult at home, too. One minute she was warm and sweet and smiling, and then, in an instant, a mood would come over her, and she would have horrible tantrums. Her initial diagnosis included ADHD, ODD, and reactive attachment disorder. That first year, which included a two-week psychiatric hospitalization, she was also diagnosed as having an anxiety disorder.

I investigated therapy for her and found a wonderfully gifted play therapist. Two years later, things had improved. LeAnn was playing softball on a team with her sister; she loved school and Girl Scouts. She had a best friend and was invited often to play at her house. We were now a family of five. We began contemplating another adoption.

James was ten when we saw his picture and heard his story. Again, we began down that difficult path of adoption. Although his diagnosis, which included ADHD, ODD, and reactive attachment disorder, sounded strikingly similar to that of our adopted daughter, his situation was more complicated from the beginning: During the time when we learned about him, he was living in a psychiatric residential treatment center for children with emotional and behavioral disorders.

Still, while LeAnn's first two years with us were rough, she was doing quite well—so we thought we were equipped and experienced enough to go a second round, even if James's problems were bigger.

We visited James, a handsome little boy with big brown eyes and a smile that could melt your heart, in the residential facility, and then we began home visits. He called us Mom and Dad within a few weeks. We fell in love with him. I tried not to get too optimistic that his problems would disappear, but when summer went like a dream, I was thrilled. He loved to go to the park and play ball. He loved cars and he loved our dogs. As summer came to an end, we made plans to have him attend a nearby private elementary school.

Overnight, everything changed. Out of the blue, he began acting wild, running around making animal noises and jumping on beds. Then one evening he scared us by leaning over the second-floor balcony of our home as if he were going to jump. I tried everything I knew to distract him, but he would not—or could not—stop. At the end of a nerve-jangling evening, he gave up; it was probably pure exhaustion that got him to come down.

Despite his difficult past, we were never told that his school records also showed that he had been extremely aggressive. We knew he had attended a special school for his behaviors, but we were naive and didn't understand the extent of his aggression. When we went to enroll him in school, we learned that he could not be maintained in a classroom of five or six children for more than an hour or two. The original school we had in mind for him was not going to work. Instead, he was placed in a special-treatment program at a school I now clearly realize was not right for him—and everything began to spiral downward from there.

One day a few weeks later, James held the family hostage in the backyard while he swung a broom over his head, striking everything in its path—us, the patio windows, the dog. Another time, he had a tantrum and began beating his own head onto the asphalt street.

Eventually, we had to place him out-of-home, and shortly after, we were confronted with a difficult decision: Our son's adoption was not yet final. We had been trying our best for twelve months to make a home for James. Could we really do this for the long haul? The staff at the residential treatment center told us we were his last chance. If we walked away, he could be in the foster care system forever. He needed a family, and we had committed to provide that for him. But there was the issue of safety—we needed our three other children to feel safe in their own home. What was the right thing to do? Friends said he was just too damaged and reassured us that nobody would blame us if we just walked away. All my husband and I could think about, though, was, *If not our family, then what family will he have in his life?*

We also knew that whatever we decided, the decision would affect our other children. If we walked away from James, would they wonder what it would take for us to walk away from them? Would LeAnn's fears of abandonment resurface? Even though we had experienced pain with James, we had also grown to love him. He was so likable and warmhearted on his good days, the days we saw the real James shining through a crack in the wall of fear and anger that usually surrounded him.

On a day that is seared in my memory, we decided to finalize the adoption while James was still in the treatment center. We hoped that if he knew we were going to adopt him—that we were in this for the long haul—he would reach a turning point. He seemed to get better initially, but every time we tried to bring him home, he would have a major setback. Things would go well for a week or so, then he would explode and get violent. We had the police and EMTs at our home so often that we knew them all by name. He went from facility to facility. He had a new doctor at every site, and a new list of medications to try. Each treatment center had a different therapy and behavior modification approach. Some of the punishment systems used seemed downright abusive to me. In one, he was dressed in scrubs and placed in a room with nothing in it. Every day that he did not show any aggression, he was given something back. He was not allowed to talk to anyone or ask for anything. He could come out only for bathroom breaks and meals at a table separate from everyone else. If he was aggressive in any way—even verbally—everything was removed from his room and he had to start over. Another treatment center had "levels" called green light, yellow light, and red light. Red light meant he was "frozen" for twenty-four hours. "Frozen" entailed sitting in a three-foot taped-off square on the floor, cross-legged, facing a wall for forty-five minutes out of every waking hour of the day. The other fifteen minutes he could do a quiet activity assigned by staff.

With time, I saw my little boy growing not only larger in size, but in anger and contempt. For three years, our son's longest period at home (other than that first summer) was thirteen consecutive days. The scariest part of this whole ordeal was that we didn't have any better ideas. I wanted James to come home and be a part of the family I had in my mind—four kids going to school together, playing sports, and having friends spend the night. I wanted family vacations and holiday celebrations spent together. I wanted all six of us to walk into church together. I didn't bargain for road trips across the state every other week for family visits to the hospital or late nights at the psych ward. I read everything I could get my hands on about his disorders and potential treatments. I was a pharmacist, and with all that I had learned about this child's care, I was well on my way to specializing in psychiatric pharmacy.

For years I had thought of James as a small child who needed our help. But now, he was different: He was growing quickly, and quickly growing more violent. I was told that at his size (five foot four, 165 pounds), the children's residential treatment facilities in our state could no longer handle him. He had assaulted several staff at his last placement, and they were afraid of him. He was placed in a state residential treatment program. The next ten months we were on a roller coaster trying to do everything the experts said to do, believing each time we tried something new, it would make the difference and he would be able to come home for good. At home, our other children had become very protective of their dad and me. They were afraid he would hurt us. For the most part, his aggression was aimed at authority figures, including me and my husband, not his peers. But I feared this could change. His sisters reached out and tried to maintain a relationship with him. Our older son, however, became very distant. He watched chaos being played and replayed in his home, and he was tired of it. He was angry and embarrassed by his brother's behavior in and around our neighborhood.

James is seventeen now, and he remains in a group home four miles from our home, a pre-independent living program. It has been a seven-year journey since we first decided to bring him into our life. I continue to ponder the question of what it means to be a family. I have come to accept the fact that we cannot change our son and that he is simply not able to function full-time at home with us. Home must be a safe place, and we cannot compromise the well-being of any member of our family. But we will always be here for him. We believe in him. During the occasional family dinners with James, and on our summer vacation, there are moments while sharing a meal or fishing on the lake that I catch glimpses of my family the way I envisioned them in the beginning, and I smile inside. Our other three children are in college now (including LeAnn, who continues to thrive), and my husband and I are quickly approaching the "empty nest" years. But the insight I had a few years ago still guides me: How I define "family" has little to do with where we eat or sleep, and everything to do with the love and commitment we feel toward one another.

Good Grief

Felice McCreary

Felice McCreary is the mother of Sophie, an eleven-year-old girl diagnosed with bipolar disorder, and Collin, a ten-year-old boy diagnosed with Tourette's syndrome and obsessive-compulsive disorder. She and her family live in Dripping Springs, Texas.

Let me begin with a warning: This is not going to be one of those happy, uplifting tales of parenthood. For me, raising two special-needs children has been a continuous process of grieving. There has been no closure to my grief. It is a perpetual spin cycle. With every milestone, with every crisis, and with every new diagnosis, the grief returns, sometimes in full force, and other times with a mild reminder that my life and my children's lives are not what my dreams once held. While I know that healing is still possible for me, I have come to accept, and be happy, even, with what I have.

I was shattered by my daughter's diagnosis of bipolar disorder seven years ago. She was four at the time. It shouldn't have been a shock, but it was. No one in my family was bipolar—my husband and I didn't even really know what that was. My expectations and dreams for my child—none of which included mental illness—were firmly intact in my mind. I envisioned myself as a stay-at-home mom, happily taking Sophie to dance class and soccer practice. I imagined us sitting on the bathroom floor painting our toenails together and running around the backyard in the evening catching fireflies. But by the time Sophie was three, she began throwing terrible tantrums—pulling drapes off the windows, breaking lamps, and running outside to hide in the woods. At first, I blamed myself. I believed it was my parenting that had caused her bad behavior. (I now realize that this was irrational, as we showered her with affection and followed the guidelines laid out in the child-care books to a tee.) My husband, Steve, and I took parenting classes through the school district and listened closely to the discipline advice doled out by well-intentioned friends and family. But nothing we did seemed to help. Then one day, after she had become angry because I wouldn't let her color on the wall, my four-year-old daughter told me she wished she could make herself go away forever. At that moment, I finally realized my child's problems were far greater than any shortcomings I might have as a parent. Sophie was not on any medications and had not been evaluated by a neurologist yet—but I knew in my heart it was time to look into both.

When you finally get a diagnosis for a child, you feel strangely up. I remember feeling optimistic: *Now we have the help we need.* Our lives could continue as I had planned, only with the addition of medication and therapy. I was happy with the thought that I could "fix" Sophie. We started her on medication—mood stabilizers for a five-year-old!—and we went through Depakote, lithium, Trileptal, and Lamictal trying to find just the right drug.

But something happened to my daughter on meds—something frightening. She morphed into a different person—and not in the ways we hoped. Sophie battled weight gain, memory loss, bouts of nausea, and dizziness. Yet we were not about to give up on meds; repeatedly, the experts we consulted told us it was the only way to stabilize her wild mood swings. Through the years, her condition worsened. She became more depressed. She was irritable and frustrated most of the time. She would scream at us without the slightest provocation. And she took all of her anger out on me. Many nights I had to lock her younger brother, Collin, in my bedroom so I could try to control Sophie as she ran after me with a baseball bat or kitchen knife. She felt so worthless and overwhelmed with her illness that, several times, she tried to end it all. One day, on the way to school, she tried to jump out of the car. And once, while we were at therapy, she ran out into the four-lane highway in hopes of getting hit by a vehicle. By this time, we had added Wellbutrin, an antidepressant, and Seroquel, an antipsychotic, to her medication. But her aggression and impulsivity never dissipated. Her moods never stabilized for more than a week at a time, and her depression deepened. The more depressed she became, the more I realized that I did not know how to help her. How do you parent a child who wants to die? No discipline could change her behavior. My constant attempts to rein her in only validated her sense of imperfection. She believed so strongly that she was a bad person that she could not believe she was loved, no matter how many times we told her so. She pushed away our affection with anger and aggression, with yelling, cussing, and hitting. The more she shoved us away, the more we tried to show we loved her. I look back now and realize that I was in the bargaining stage of grief. I told myself: *The more I love her, the better she will get.* But each new problem or trauma reminded me that her illness was not going away.

Then I myself hit depression. Steve struggled, too. His own dream of a family didn't entail his son calling him hysterically because his sister was trying to hit his mommy with a baseball bat. We hid our kitchen knives and baseball bats. We took classes through the National Association of Mental Illness to learn how to restrain our daughter without hurting her or ourselves.

Without anything closely resembling a "normal" home life, my son, Collin, suffered, too. Through therapy, we learned he had post-traumatic stress syndrome from living in crisis at such a young age. We were not able to fully comprehend his troubles until months later, however, when he was diagnosed with Tourette's syndrome and obsessive-compulsive disorder (OCD).

The high of thinking I could fix my daughter, then my son, then my own depression—followed by the low that I could not—was almost too much to bear. We had to admit it: Sophie's illness had become too big for all of us. One night, in her misery, Sophie, now age eight, almost succeeded in ending her life. I guess she had just had enough. While I was cooking dinner she became very angry. (At times her anger seemed to appear out of nowhere. To this day, I have never fully understood what precipitated her anger that evening.) She started throwing the food I was preparing on the floor. When I tried to stop her, she hit me. I ran to the bedroom to call my husband, and she ran after me and ripped the phone cord out of the wall. Collin and I headed for the bathroom and locked the door, which really angered Sophie. She grabbed a croquet mallet and started rapping on the bathroom door. When we didn't come out she started banging the blunt end of the stick on her head. Minutes later, I came out of the bathroom to try to protect her from herself. She ran to the garage and grabbed the bleach bottle. I remember feeling like we were both suspended in time. She didn't move. I was too scared to even twitch. As she brought the bleach to her mouth, I screamed and lunged to grab the bottle. She managed to pour it on her head as she fell to the floor in sheer exhaustion.

These last years have sparked much soul-searching, and I suppose that is the silver lining. In an effort to regain control over our lives, my husband and I placed our daughter in an out-of-state residential treatment center (RTC), so our whole family could get therapy and try to recover from the chaos in our home. Agreeing to let go of your kids is complicated. Not only does it force you to accept the gravity of your child's illness and recognize the effect it is having on everyone, but it also forces everyone in your family to face their own vulnerability.

Sophie stayed in the RTC for twenty-three months. We visited her every six weeks for counseling and family time. Hope eventually came back into our lives. Not the hope we used to dream of, but a new, powerful kind of hope that would allow us to be the parents our children needed us to be. My son is getting treatment as well. His conditions have improved with medication and therapy. During the months my daughter was gone, I came to realize that as difficult as it is for my husband and me to deal with bipolar disorder, it is more difficult for my daughter. My preteen daughter needs me more than I need my dreams. Through the years, my grief was based on what we were not able to do as a family. I have now begun to accept our reality and look at what we *can* and *will* do.

A Truly Unique Ride

Lisa Lori

Lisa Lori is the mother of three boys—Zachary, age five; Luke, age three; and Griffin, age two. At thirty-three, Lisa was diagnosed with the autoimmune disease myasthenia gravis; her children face a variety of physical challenges. They live in Old Greenwich, Connecticut.

I wish I could tell you what my sons' diagnoses are (that's not a typo—I mean all three of my children), but, unfortunately, my children don't have diagnoses. I am in the unique position of trying to figure out what exactly is wrong with them, as well as deal with parenting three children who each have physical and emotional challenges. I am not completely in the dark—when my husband and I decided to have children, it was a decision we took very seriously. I have myasthenia gravis (MG), an autoimmune disease in which the immune system creates antibodies to a particular nerve receptor at the neuromuscular junction. It is as though the receptor were a foreign protein, like a virus. The result is severe muscle weakness, characterized by drooping eyelids, a frowning or sagging mouth, and an inability to raise ones arms. Although I was assured by many experts that I could not pass my disease to my children, we have spent the last five-plus years trying to figure out how exactly my disease has affected them.

When I gave birth to my first son, Zachary, there was a quiet in the room. They knew immediately that something wasn't right. We were told that Zack failed his Apgar test and needed to be evaluated to determine what was wrong. Even after we learned that he was suffering from MG-related symptoms, we were optimistic because it was—and still is—believed that children born to women who have MG might have some symptoms initially, but it always burned out of their system within the first couple of years. Zachary's issues at birth were significant: an inability to swallow, low muscle tone, poor sucking ability. The muscle tone in his face in particular was so compromised he could not close his mouth. Leaving the hospital four days later without my child was one of the most chilling experiences of my life, but we felt confident about the future, and we knew that there was a light at the end of the tunnel. As the weeks wore on and his condition did not improve, however, our shock inched toward horror.

Zachary spent five long weeks in the neonatal intensive care unit. While his condition was unchanged after that time, it was stable, so the doctors told us that we could bring him home—with the proper training and medical equipment. They told us not to worry, that it couldn't last much longer. I remember feeling numb while we were trained at the hospital on how to insert a feeding tube, use a feeding machine and heart monitor, and conduct baby CPR. I became aware of how serious our situation was: If I made a mistake, I could drown my own son with milk. Regardless, we were ecstatic to bring him home on Christmas Eve of that year and be free of the hospital.

After dinner, my husband was changing Zack's diaper in our bedroom when he called for me to please come and help him. Zack had pulled out the feeding tube that was inserted in his nose. We were told to expect this, but so soon after we came home? We were also told to reinsert it right away, as he needed to have it in at all times because feedings are so frequent. Zack screamed and I cried as I reinserted the tube. My husband and I prayed that I would do it correctly.

That first week with Zack at home was a roller coaster. So began our new routine. Between his feeding tube and the machine that monitored his breathing at night, we were constantly on edge. The monitor would sound an alarm almost every time he moved his foot—I wasn't sure who would have a heart attack first, him or me. In the end, we had to unplug the machine so we could all get some sleep—and pray he wouldn't stop breathing—giving new meaning to "restless sleep."

Every two weeks, Zack had a series of blood tests to determine if the antibody count in his blood was lowering. These antibodies in his system—from the MG in my system—were making him weak and unable to perform the simple and yet very complicated functions of eating and swallowing. After eight weeks, he remained the same, and I thought, *My god, he might never eat on his own. What will I do?* And so, when he was two months old, we took the first of many medical "risks," on the advice of his neurologist, and cleaned out the plasma from his body and replaced it with new plasma. Since his own body was not producing the antibody to his nerve receptors—the cause of MG—the doctors said he should begin to improve, and he did—slowly. At fourteen weeks, we finally removed the tube from his nose and fed him a whole bottle for the first time. At fourteen months, I saw him take his first awkward steps within just a few weeks of being able to crawl. While other toddlers were smiling and saying "Mommy" at exactly the right point when a new mother is exhausted and needs to bond, my child could physically do neither. Still, even though our milestones weren't found in parenting magazines, we celebrated them all the same.

For the next few months I floated through my life in a fog, unable to explain my circumstances, unable to understand what or why it was happening. I spent countless hours on the floor with physical, occupational, and speech therapists while they worked with Zack. Months passed, and we were shocked at how slow the progress was. *Why wasn't this going away?* The doctors we talked to seemed to agree that my son's illness was a freak coincidence.

And so I had two more children—one that we tried to conceive;

the other, honestly, quite by surprise. With these next two pregnan-
cies, I, too, had my plasma cleaned out every two weeks to rid myself of the disease, but my next two boys were born with the same
symptoms as Zachary, although they were slightly less severe. The
disappointment was profound and almost more painful to take than
the first experience. We had a lot of very smart people scratching
their heads—*Hmm, we've never seen this before*. I must have recited
my case to one hundred doctors and residents those first few years;
every one wanted to take a look at us. While my kids became famous, I grew weary. Lots of questions, very few answers.

When Zack was three, I begged his nursery school to let him stay,
despite his drooling. "It's going to go away," I told them. I still believed it then. (His school relented.) He began to say a few words
around this time, and within a few weeks, sentences came. Honestly,
it freaked me out a little. It was as if his brain had been absorbing all
of the therapy, but his body had not been able to respond, and then,
presto, it happened. Progress was slow, but when things like this happened, the future seemed hopeful. The most pervasive problem that
remained was the low facial tone and his inability to close his mouth,
which seriously complicated his speech. I started to think that, one
day, I would just tell him to close his mouth, and as soon as he could
understand what I meant, he would do it.

When Zack was about four and a half years old and he still could
not close his mouth, still could not control his drooling, and only
about 50 percent of his speech was intelligible, I finally realized that
his physical problems were not going to go away. Zack is now five
and a half, and Luke is three and a half, and they cannot close their
mouths at all. My youngest son, Griffin, can close his—sometimes.
Because they can't close their mouths, excessive fluid builds up in
their ears, which for a while caused significant hearing loss (com-
pounding their speech problems). We often thought our sons were

ignoring us when we spoke to them over the past few years; more than likely, though, they just didn't hear us.

They have gone so long without closing their mouths now that their upper palates have become extremely narrow, and they cannot make several sounds. And in an even stranger twist of fate, because their palates are so narrow, they can no longer bite down properly to close their mouths. It is not physically possible for my sons to say certain words, no matter how much speech therapy they have. Speech therapists don't like to hear this; many think if we hold enough tongue depressors between their lips and push their lips closed with our hands, someday they will close their mouths. My Zachary is a very bright little boy—he can read, count to one hundred, tell you what the capitol of California is, but he cannot make his lips close together or keep the water from flowing from his mouth for all the chocolate bars in the world.

As I watch my boys go about their lives, I have come to believe that they are prisoners inside their own bodies. I have also come to believe that I am the only person who understands them completely. My husband and I are a team—I am the coach, and he is the cheerleader. He supports me and understands that I have a special bond with them, and he tries to keep my spirits up when it becomes overwhelming. We remind each other constantly that we are doing the best we can, and that more than anything, we need to give our sons a good home life. I know that I am extremely lucky to have him for a partner.

My children and I have developed a language and communications system all our own. We have learned sign language, to get us through some of the rough patches. When I separate from them for playdates, school, or camp, I am not just leaving them as a parent, but as a translator. They have learned, at a very young age, that, in the end, they will have to become their own advocates. Strangers often ask, *What is wrong with them? Are they autistic?* Sometimes the questions are friendly, and sometimes they are not so polite. Sometimes people who are curious won't meet my eyes.

Even I want to cringe when I hear Zack repeat something three or four times at Little League practice, without being understood. I am sad when a boy asks me why they are always frowning. I smile when people tell me how patient Zack is while they try to understand him. It seems he has no place to go but to wait for his body and his face to catch up with the rest of him. Luke is the opposite. He is self-conscious. He won't even try to speak when other people are around. He knows the risks involved. He will go a whole year in a music class that he loves without ever saying a word. Recently, when he was trying to tell me something and I said, "I'm sorry, I don't understand," he took my breath away when he said, "But I'm talking to you!" I knelt down and hugged him with joy.

Three months ago, a very famous doctor who was recommended to me by the National Institutes of Health agreed to take on our case, to help us understand what happened so we might be able to develop a treatment going forward. But in my heart, I know the road ahead. There will be pain and some bullying. There will be kindness and victories. I don't want my children to be normal anymore. I already believe they are extraordinary; I am reminded of it in ways big and small every single day.

SECTION 4

Schools That Work,
Schools That Don't

I magine uprooting your family, selling your home, and moving to a small apartment five minutes away, all because your child needs to be in a special-needs classroom—and the board of education can't accept applications from children who reside just blocks outside the district.

Or, try to imagine sending your child to a residential treatment center for two years—your firstborn, the one you pictured playing baseball with after school?

Or picture this: You hear through a friend who teaches at the local elementary school that your son's teacher walked into the teacher's lounge the first day of school and announced to the staff with a scowl, "Damn, they stuck me with that autistic kid."

These are the kinds of moments when, as a parent, you are forced to become an advocate for your child. In collecting their stories, the parents in this section often told me that they weren't exactly born with the "advocacy" gene; it was something they acquired as their children grew up and had to make their way through the world.

Every parent brings a different sensibility to his or her role as advocate. Take Drusilla Belman, the mother of Henry in "Expect the

Best—It Just Might Happen to You." What made Drusilla and her husband, Albert, put out the FOR SALE sign on their gorgeous Brooklyn home? "The pain of seeing my copper-haired, glasses-wearing kid—who is delightful and funny and friendly—not fit in or act like other children shot through my body daily," she explains. After seven months of desperately needing a school change and groveling for it with the New York City Department of Education, Drusilla writes, "[I learned that] sometimes I will have to wage war for him [Henry], even if it gets bloody." And so it goes: Without a guidebook or guru beside them to offer just the right advice during moments like this, the parents in this section trusted their gut, to wing it, to take risks. And they all succeeded.

It wasn't easy, though. Finding the right fit is not so simple when it comes to kids with special needs. I learned this the hard way. Each option we considered for Toby—small classroom, big school, private or public—took phone calls, interviews, meet-and-greets, paperwork. Then there was the question of whether there was even room for him at the place we loved—a public school just blocks from our home, with four teachers in the classroom, soundproof walls to limit noise, and an occupational therapy staff trained to deal with sensory disorders. Getting him in took months of testing, meetings, and calls. But there was a silver lining: It gave us valuable knowledge about our son's strengths and weaknesses and, ultimately, led us to the proper classroom environment for him. We learned that he excelled when he worked in a quiet place, with teachers who were patient but persistent and who were masters of structure, but not martinets. After months of refusing to dance or sing in class, in the winter of his kindergarten year, he began participating—a first for a kid who despises noise. I watched in awe as he pulled a practice CD of winter concert songs out of his backpack one evening and happily belted out the tunes while my babysitter made dinner. (Turns out he has a pretty decent voice!) The singing, the dancing, the happiness—none of it would have happened in a different classroom. I am convinced that if we had taken one Kierkegaardian leap of faith into the first school that offered him a seat, he would be sitting in silence in music class today.

Before we even began our hunt for the perfect school (and before we realized the extent of Toby's sensory issues), Toby had been enrolled in a local preschool. I knew that this was the wrong school for him, though, when his teachers reported all too often that he was quiet, not engaged with the class, and not really trying his hardest to make friends or learn new skills. His wasn't a behavior problem—quite the opposite. He had made himself invisible (not tough to do in a class of twenty rowdy five-year-olds). It took all our strength and conviction to pull him out midyear and place him in an inclusion classroom in another school (one where he could get special services and more attention from teachers but still participate in a regular classroom day). Administrators at the preschool he was attending did not support the idea of yanking him from his classroom. And they balked at the idea of us pushing him ahead into kindergarten, particularly in the middle of the year. It was a risk, but my husband and I agreed: We knew our son best. We knew he was extremely bright and fairly bored—he could handle kindergarten half a year early. And he certainly wasn't losing much by leaving his current class. By spring, just a few months after the switch, Toby was engaged in his kindergarten class activities and was even making friends.

In the fourth contribution in this section, Dawn Mazzeo, also from Brooklyn, remembers being in desperate need of a place where her nine-year-old son, Noah, could learn to manage his feelings as well as his schoolwork. His life was split between holding it together at school and letting his anger and anxiety loose at home. When they find Andrus, the "just right school" for Noah, Dawn writes about how she cannot believe how calm her house felt—and how, as her daughter and husband relaxed, they all began to enjoy one another's company again. Her story confirmed for me the interconnectedness of school and home: If one block is teetering precariously in your life, the whole stack can come crashing down.

Often, the right school proves to be the key to unlocking a child's spirit. Schools teach math and writing and science, but they also teach confidence, manners, conflict resolution, and patience. For a child like my son, or any other special-needs kids in this book, to be a success, they need to learn that their default setting cannot be defiant, angry, or overly shy.

This section is, by no means, a complete picture of the types of schools that exist in this country for special-needs children. Nor do I think it shows the full breadth of problems children with mental health issues face in academia. But it will open (or reopen) your eyes to the idea that school can be almost as important as home life. You are your child's first teacher, of course, but the lessons your child takes home from his classroom after an eight-hour day, five days a week, will surely make a meaningful difference.

"I Got That Autistic Kid"

Patti Gaultney

Patti Gaultney is the mother of Wesley, a seventeen-year-old boy diagnosed with autism at age four. She and her family live in Santa Barbara, California.

Imagine this: On your son's first day of second grade, his new teacher walks into the teachers' lounge, sits down, and says to a fellow staffer, "Damn, they stuck me with that autistic kid." This is the way my son's teacher—the woman with whom he would be spending five days a week for the next year—reacted to having my little boy in her class. Another teacher and friend overheard the exchange and reported it back to me.

It was as if Wesley had a red-inked label of autism boldly stamped across his forehead. He wasn't seen as a real, live person—a person with potential.

The teacher refused to bend in any way to help Wesley learn. At my husband's and my first meeting with her, I asked if we could implement "priming" with Wesley. (Priming is a strategy in which a child is introduced to the class work in a relaxed home atmosphere before it's presented in school, so the child can be acclimated to the material and therefore less anxious and better able to focus when the material is presented in school.) She said priming was impossible—that even *she* didn't know in advance what she would be teaching. She offered no compromises, no discussion, only a flat no.

We soon realized that it wasn't that Wesley's teacher didn't know what she was going to teach in advance. As worksheets came home, we noticed that the copyright dates were twenty years old. She knew what she was going to teach—the exact same thing she had been teaching for twenty years. She simply did not want to be bothered with a special-needs child. Unfortunately, Wesley made little academic progress that year.

We were optimistic, however, as Wesley began third grade. His elderly teacher seemed sweet, but we soon discovered that she, too, had preconceived notions about the worth of special-needs students versus her "real" students. Outside the classroom, there were even more challenges. Wesley didn't know how to make friends or how to judge the quality of friendships. In his desperation to connect, he mistook the attention of a group of bullies for friends. One day, he arrived home from school with a plate-size dark bruise on his back. I immediately took him back to school and showed it to the school nurse and principal. The principal merely shrugged his shoulders and announced, "Boys will be boys." The bullying persisted. As third grade progressed, Wesley was talked out of his lunch, money, jacket, and backpack.

One evening when Wesley was eight, Wesley's third-grade teacher called. She asked, in her sweet, singsongy voice, if we had heard about the incident at school. "What incident?" I asked, as the hairs on the back of my neck began to prickle. After speaking with her for a while, it became clear that while the children were waiting for the bus, Wesley started to question the ringleader, repeating his question over and over. During this time, Wesley's verbal perseverance, a common trait of autism, was in full swing. Annoyed, the ringleader and his friends forced Wesley into the bathroom, stuck his head into the toilet, and flushed.

My mind raced when I heard that. *Why had no one called from the school? What was going on?* Then came her next question: "I was wondering," she asked, "if Wesley would write the boy a letter of apology for annoying him."

I could barely believe I heard her correctly. *Did she really say that?* My mind was whirling. I finally muttered, "I don't think so," and slammed down the phone.

I ran into Wesley's room where he was playing with his trains. I needed to hug him, to make sure he was okay. I wanted to assure him that nothing like this would ever happen again.

That day, my husband and I decided that Wesley would change school districts. I could no longer avoid conflict by not challenging authority, a habit I have struggled with over the years. I grew up in an alcoholic household where questioning authority had horrendous consequences—but now, for my own child, the stakes were just too high. Wesley needed a protector, an advocate. I had to make people look past the label and see the beauty, potential, and soul of my child. Our search for a new school was different than those of other parents, parents who considered test scores and extracurricular activities in making their choice. My search was based on intangibles—an attitude of acceptance, a welcoming spirit, a competent staff who had high expectations of all their students, as well as a student population that accepted atypical children.

We are fortunate to have found such a school. At our first meeting with the principal, psychologist, special-education teacher, and regular-education teacher, we knew we were at the right place. It was a charming school, built in the twenties; its pink walls and tiled roof exuded warmth. The psychologist asked me if I had heard of priming, and suggested that we use it. I was floored—the very thing that the previous school had denied was being suggested before I even brought it up. She also told me about the "friendship club" she ran, where every few weeks she brought together a small group of children, both typical and atypical, who had difficulty in making friends, and taught them how to form good friendships. Lessons Wesley gleaned from friendship club—such as making small talk—still benefit him to this day.

Wesley made his first good friend, José, at the new school as well. José was very small for his age, with bright brown eyes, a crooked grin, and ears that he'd not quite grown into yet. José accepted Wesley at the same time that he nudged him toward "typical" behavior. José convinced him that crying at minor incidents was not "cool."

Finally, Wesley's regular-education teacher had a background in special education and graciously catered to his special needs. When she saw that he was zoning out, she would gently place a hand on his shoulder or call out his name to bring him back into focus.

After the first year at his new school, Wesley's math skills jumped three grade levels. Other talents started to emerge as well, and the kids began to not only accept Wesley, but to respect him. He had an uncanny knowledge of geography, and the kids would turn to Wesley to help them locate obscure African countries on the class globe. By the time he was in fifth grade, he had started to run track and was one of the fastest runners at the school.

Was his school experience perfect? No. His reading skills only slowly inched forward. (Later, we discovered techniques to help him overcome his severe dyslexia.) And I still remember the day when I walked on campus and saw Wesley in the middle of a group of his sixth-grade peers, all of them laughing together. My heart leaped at the sight. However, as I came closer, I heard various kids yell out to Wesley, "Say 'yellow'"—then laugh when he said "leyoo." Wesley, in his innocence, did not realize he was being teased, but I, as a mom, surely felt the sting. However, the overall trajectory of Wesley's life would have been completely different if we had not found a school that accepted him—or, I should say, embraced him.

Over the next few years, I realized that I would always need to speak up for Wesley's rights, to make others aware of his uniqueness, to combat intolerance and demand that he receive the education he was entitled to. Moreover, with each small victory, I became stronger, not only in advocating for my son, but for other children as well. I demanded that Wesley be treated as an individual and not as a label—not as "that autistic boy."

Would Wesley turn out to be a typical teenager? My husband and I never dreamed of that possibility during his early years—but he is. He runs competitively on his high school cross-country and track teams, and he is taking a full load of regular-education classes, including precalculus and chemistry. He's actively involved in his faith community, and although it was difficult at first, he has begun to venture out on youth group outings and mission trips.

That "autistic boy"? His name is Wesley, and we are incredibly proud of him.

Expect the Best—
It Just Might Happen to You

Drusilla Belman

*Drusilla is the mother of Henry, who is six years old
and has sensory issues and speech delays. She and
her family live in Brooklyn, New York.*

We are moving in three weeks, from a five-bedroom house
with a brand-new deck and a flower-filled garden to a small
rental apartment five minutes away. We have lived in our house for
three years and have finally become friends with a few of our neighbors. My husband, Albert, and I don't want to move, but we have to.
Our six-year-old son, Henry, is going into kindergarten, and he needs
to be in an inclusion class—a classroom that mixes special-ed and
mainstream children, and is taught by both a regular teacher and a
teacher trained in special education. Not all public schools in Brooklyn have inclusion classrooms, and the ones that do are in high demand. In order to even apply for one of these coveted spots, we
need to be in the correct school district.

Our current district had a couple of schools with inclusion classrooms, but, after touring these schools, I knew immediately that they
were not an option for Henry. The hallways were long, drab tunnels,
heavily coated in institutional gray; the schools' test scores were well
below average. Ten blocks south of us, however, was District 15,
which had three bright and airy, well-performing schools with great
inclusion programs; we could see the district from our bedroom window, but we were locked out.

I should interrupt this lesson on Brooklyn schools to tell you a little bit about Henry. Henry is my copper-haired, glasses-wearing kid—who is delightful and funny and friendly. People say he reminds them of that boy in *Jerry Maguire* who talks about how bunnies can smell fear. He is bursting with information about everything, from animals to planets, and he is constantly asking questions about his world. Adults find him particularly charming because he treats them as his equal, taking a hand in conversations and speaking enthusiastically about his family, school, and sports. But he can also be quirky and rigid and afraid—a lot. He's been this way since he was a baby. After several evaluations, we now know that he has sensory integration disorder, that he is overly sensitive to his environment. He has always had a tremendous fear of loud noises—a fire drill at school would cause a fit of screaming, and God forbid the toilet flushes automatically in a public restroom. Then there is his extreme reluctance to go from one activity to another; when it comes to transitions, he needs to be prepared well in advance. Even if all of his friends are off to the playground, Henry would rather stay where he is than move on to the next activity.

Henry was two when my mother gently suggested that he be evaluated for speech delay. Four years later, Henry is still doing speech and occupational therapy. The progress is slow, and he doesn't always want to participate. There have been times when he asks why he has to go and other kids don't. I have lost patience with a therapist or two who couldn't explain how bouncing on a huge ball or playing with a frog-shaped beanbag was going to cure Henry's fear of carousels. The connection between what therapists do for him physically and emotionally is sometimes hard to decipher, but I have learned not to question the process.

I did a lot of questioning about his education, however. The months before our big real-estate decision went something like this: First, tour the local private schools. Getting your kid into private school in New York City is often the first major challenge of their little lives. I've known people who put their kids on the waiting list for *pre-school* when they first found out they were pregnant. Private elementary is even more competitive—each school gets thousands of applications per year, for eighteen- to twenty-thousand-dollar spaces in the kindergarten class. Two of the admissions directors at these schools were honest and told me that they just didn't have the resources for special-needs children—however, we were welcome to apply. (Frankly, I didn't want to give them the chance to reject him or us, and I told myself they didn't offer what he needed.)

Next, we visited a neuropsychologist who, after four months on her waiting list, confirmed what Albert and I intuitively knew: that Henry would benefit from an inclusion classroom. This conclusion came after she gave Henry five mornings of tests and wrote an extensive report that explained so many of his quirky behaviors. It was a glorious experience to have a professional define Henry's condition so accurately and to tell us that he could overcome his quirks with therapy and the right school environment.

Now I just had to focus on finding the right public school for Henry. Just ten blocks away from our home, PS 321 in Park Slope is one of the highest-rated public elementary schools in the city—and known to have a wonderful inclusion team. After doing a bit of research, I learned that, by far, PS 321 would be the best place for Henry. I also learned that there were only three inclusion seats remaining—with an angry, anxious mob of parents fighting for them. My mission was to secure one of these seats for Henry.

The person at the New York City Department of Education in Brooklyn in charge of assigning special-ed kids to classrooms was a man named Harry Barker*—or, as Albert and I like to call him, God. As soon as I decided that PS 321 was the best option for Henry—

---

*A pseudonym.

almost a year before Henry was to begin kindergarten—I called Harry. He told me it would be many months before he assigned placements but that I should continue touring schools in the meantime. He also told me that PS 321 was the most popular school in District 15 and that there weren't enough spots for the families already in the zone. Harry said I could call him with questions anytime.

So call him I did—methodically, every Monday morning. I left messages all through the winter, always polite and entreating. Harry would call me back every so often to say he had no news, that everything would be sorted out by the beginning of June. Finally, June arrived; by this point, the pressure was mounting, as Henry needed to start kindergarten that September. I woke up every morning at four thirty with one thought: How will this nightmare end? I'd wait until six to wake Albert, then make him go over backup plans. Plan A: We beg and plead with the principal at 321 for a variance (meaning the school allows him to go there even though we live in a different district); in this case, we celebrate in the streets. We knew that PS 321 was in such high demand, though, that a variance would be highly unlikely. Plan B: We push all summer to get him into a special-education private school. I had never visited any of these schools, but I knew there were two good ones in the Manhattan—although one had a two-year waiting list and the other was thirty thousand dollars a year. This seemed extreme, knowing that, just a short walk from our house, was 321, filled with friends and neighbors, which had a program recommended to us by a psychologist we trusted. Plan C: We sell our house and move to the suburbs where we were told that many public schools have great special-ed programs. It was Plan C I dreaded most. Albert and I had spent many hours debating which would be worse: my spending my entire day in a metallic-silver minivan or him commuting to his investment bank on the 6:18 train with the *Wall Street Journal*–carrying crowd, getting home after the kids were asleep. I was raised in New York City, and the whole suburban lifestyle sounded so unfamiliar; Albert came from a suburb of Philly and had hoped not to go back. And yet, we both knew that if moving out of town were the best thing for Henry—if the alternative was staying in a bad school situation—we would move in a heartbeat.

It was one of those final early-summer mornings that I shed my playground Pumas and got all dolled up, bought a box of cookies, and went down to actually introduce myself to Harry, in hopes that a face-to-face conversation might produce more fruitful results. The New York City Department of Education was in downtown Brooklyn. The office itself was a crazy maze of cubicles and cramped offices that reminded me of interrogation rooms that you see in crime dramas on TV. I was ushered into his office. After seventy-five previous conversations, I could have picked Harry out of a lineup. He was in his fifties, graying and disheveled, very Oscar Madison–like. But his most memorable and familiar characteristic was his endearingly extreme Brooklyn accent. "Howaya, Mrs. B?" he asked upon shaking my hand. I told him what I'd seen, what I hoped for, and how much it meant to me. Suddenly, standing there in his office, with files piled everywhere and notes scribbled all over the manila covers, it hit me how exhausting this whole process had been, and how much I detested begging and nagging everyone, from the tour guides and security guards at each school to the secretaries and principals—but most of all, this very kind, overworked man. I fought it, but my eyes filled with tears. It was then that Harry leaned forward and said, "Mrs. B, I gotta be honest with you. There is a ball game going on in the stadium, and your son is sitting in the parking lot." That's when the anvil fell from the sky. I finally understood that there would be no variance. No exceptions.

As I ran from Harry's office at the Department of Education I called Albert to say that it was clear we had to sell our house and move to PS 321's district; there was no other choice. Thankfully, Albert was totally in sync. He quickly found us a rental online, and we put our beautiful house on the market the next day. I went back to Harry's office a week later with an electricity bill from our new apartment, so he would have proof that we were legally zoned for placement. Then I waited for the news. After all, we had made the great sacrifice, now it was up to the powers that be to do the right thing by my boy. Two weeks later Harry did finally call and explained that there were more children than expected who were clamoring for all the inclusion spaces in District 15, especially for 321. We were number six on the waiting list. Two of the schools in District 15 were already filled—all was not lost, but it didn't look good. As a consolation, he said that if Henry didn't get a seat, I could spend my summer calling him every day to see if a seat had opened up for any reason.

I spent that night flipping through my two-inch-thick folder marked HENRY SCHOOLS, looking for any detail I had overlooked. Was there a person I hadn't consulted or a school that I could consider again? That Friday was Henry's last day of preschool. I already missed the nurturing, inclusive synagogue preschool that had become our family over the last three years. On my way to his classroom at the end of the day, I was thinking about how I'd somehow screwed it all up. Even though, rationally, I knew I had done everything I could, I still felt that I had missed a step, or was too late in accepting that the variance was never going to come. Maybe we were selfish for not relinquishing our beloved urban lifestyle. I couldn't shake the feeling that, at a time when Henry needed me most to be his champion, I had failed him.

And then my cell phone rang. I heard Harry's voice say, "Mrs. B, I'd like to awfah yaw son Henry a seat at PS 321." I just about combusted. After seven months of praying for this very call, and groveling for it, I simply sobbed. Then, from the other end of the line: "I'll take that as a yes."

It's been a couple of months since that call, and once or twice a day I get a pinch-me feeling, a wave of excitement and gratitude.

Henry is loving his kindergarten class at 321, and thriving there. He is getting the therapy he needs at school, mostly in groups with his new friends. We've settled into our new neighborhood and are happy to report that we are already having the neighbors over.

When I look back on my Great Kindergarten Experience and ask myself, *What did I learn?* the lesson is clear to me: I am my child's advocate, and sometimes I will have to wage war for him, even if it gets bloody—because there is nothing so deeply gratifying as doing the right thing for your bright, limited, loving, apprehensive, wonderful child.

My Friends Are Waiting for Me

Rebecca Stern

Rebecca Stern is the mother of Caleb, a five-year-old preschooler diagnosed with autism. She and her family live in Carrboro, North Carolina.

It's no easy thing to find the right school for your child—but it can transform your child's life. In the fall of 2005, my only child, Caleb, went from a self-contained classroom he shared with six other children with autism to a mainstream classroom with nineteen typically developing peers. In his new school, the Little School of Hillsborough, in Hillsborough, North Carolina, Caleb is thriving—he loves his friends and is loved in return. So that others might have a similar experience, I want to tell Caleb's story and recount how he ended up at this wonderful school, which seemed to fall from the sky like a gift from God when we were in despair.

In 2003, when Caleb was three years old, I enrolled him in a mainstream preschool program in Chapel Hill, North Carolina, that came highly recommended by several friends. For the first month, Caleb cried all day in distress and terror. Not yet understanding his disability, I was mystified and distraught. Why could he not follow the teachers' simple directions ("Caleb, it's time to clean up now") or answer direct questions ("Where is your coat?"), when he did these things at home with his father and me? Why couldn't he even begin to muster a response when a peer approached him and asked to play? Eventually, he managed to hold back his tears while at school, but he spent the day alone, as far from the other children as possible, locked in a few repetitive actions, like pushing a toy car around the sink in the "housekeeping" center. Fortunately, the school's director persuaded me to have him evaluated by our public school district's pre-K intervention team, and that is how we landed at Lincoln Center, a self-contained classroom for children with special needs, provided by the Chapel Hill/Carrboro City Schools. The school was minutes from our home, free, and he was given speech and occupational therapy services twice weekly, as indicated on his individual education plan (IEP). There we met Miss Emily.

Emily is one of those teachers with a gift. I don't mean that she's overly organized, or that she is creative or flexible or passionate about her work, although she is all of those things. I mean that she talks to children with autism, from the most mildly affected to the most severely impaired, in the same way she talks to any and every other child—with respect, concern, firmness, compassion, and love. The effect of her approach is that children in her classroom feel proud of their accomplishments and begin to perform at a level of proficiency that had seemed unattainable before. Children who have shown either no interest in school or outright dread of school actually start to look forward to it each day, because they will get to see Miss Emily there. In her care, in a classroom of only five children, my son learned that school could be fun. No longer frightened by the combined sounds of fifteen children (the number in his previous school), he could attend to what was happening around him and enjoy himself. He could follow verbal directions easily because his system was no longer overloaded. At that point in his development, he needed a classroom exactly like that: highly structured, with clear routines, and with very few children. By the end of his second year at that school, the bright, goofy, cheerful, and slightly mischievous boy we had always seen at home was beginning to show himself with his classmates. Then it was time to transition from pre-K to kindergarten, and the nightmare began.

During the summer before he was to begin prekindergarten, the district's director of special services decided (for reasons that we still cannot fathom) that Caleb should be assigned to the self-contained autism room in one of our district's elementary schools, where he would have one classmate. Historically, the children assigned to this room were either minimally verbal or nonverbal. Meanwhile, Caleb was talking up a storm at home and commenting on every passing road sign in his newfound enthusiasm for all the letters of the alphabet. We argued, marshaled evidence, submitted letters from Caleb's therapists, and ultimately went before a state-appointed mediator, but all to no avail. The district wouldn't budge. We panicked and started the search for a private school.

I began the process with a great deal of hope. After all, we weren't expecting any schools to alter their educational program or to provide extra support to Caleb. To our delight, Emily (having left the public school district to become a private tutor) had agreed to be Caleb's aide the following year, so we knew we could assure prospective schools that the teacher needn't be concerned about shortchanging other children because of Caleb's needs for individual attention. We just needed a school willing to take a kid with autism. If Caleb feels overwhelmed, he might zone out or shut down, but he doesn't act out, so no one needed to worry about aggressive or disruptive behavior. We figured: *Here's a kid with a sunny personality, who loves books, trains, trucks, and music. He's an enthusiastic learner. Plus, he has his own aide, employed by the parents. Surely we will find a good fit.*

I called church schools, private day-care centers, and very expensive private pre-K–12 schools. We were turned down at every single one—and not after thoughtful and deliberate reflection, but with one standard, nonnegotiable answer: "We aren't equipped to handle his needs." (The winner for callousness, I thought, was, "We have to consider the well-being of the other children.") These decisions were meted out without anyone involved having met our son. They thought they knew him, I suppose; they thought they knew autism. When I thought of Caleb—who knows all the words to just about any Bruce Springsteen or Cat Stevens or Stevie Wonder song, not to mention the name of every instrument in an orchestra, including the four different kinds of saxophones and the contrabassoon, this boy who says things like, "This is so nice, all eating in the dining room together!"—it just didn't add up. *This* was the kid that no school was willing to take?

So when Emily told us about a flyer she saw on a coffee-shop bulletin board for a brand-new place called the Little School, guided by the principles of Reggio Emilia, I was too worn down to feel excited or curious. Reggio Emilia is a small town in Italy where a group of parents founded a small school shortly after World War II, based on the idea that all children are natural research scientists. In practical terms, this means that the curriculum is child driven; if the children express an interest in gardening, the next several weeks are then devoted to gardening; teachers develop the theme through art, story, song, and direct experience. Reggio Emilia schools also believe in recording the child's learning faithfully, rather than through adult summaries; verbatim transcripts of children's discussions adorn the classroom. In Caleb's class, one child's passion for drawing trains evolved into a whole-class mural that took weeks to complete, and which now hangs, magnificent and framed, in the school's entrance. (Today, acolytes of Reggio make pilgrimages to the town where it all began.) Last summer we knew none of this, of course. As I mentioned, I was too dispirited to even make an inquiry.

My husband, slightly less weathered by the whole experience, did call the school, which was in the next town over, and reached one of its two directors, Christa Niven. Briefly, he summed up our situation: Our son has autism, we want a regular classroom, and he will have his own aide. I will never forget Christa's immediate response: "This sounds like a win-win!" My husband and I were so shell-shocked that it literally took weeks before we really believed that this school was not only willing to take Caleb, but that they actually were excited about taking him. Both directors believe wholeheartedly in inclusion, so they were pleased to welcome a kid like Caleb to their new community. Practically in a daze, I visited the school and completed all the necessary enrollment forms. I learned that the directors had founded it because of their dissatisfaction with the schooling choices available for their own children. They had a vision of a community in which children were celebrated for their unique selves. I'll also never forget my first phone conversation with the school's other director, Jennifer Dock, in which I hesitantly mentioned an aspect of Caleb's sensory integrative dysfunction—"He might get alarmed at the prospect of touching anything goopy or gloppy or sticky," I said.

"Oh, yeah," Jennifer replied, "one of my favorite kids in my old classroom really hated the way the tops of new socks felt on his legs."

It turns out that Jennifer had taught in a classroom for children with behavioral and emotional disorders, but a lot of children on the autism spectrum ended up in her class, too. What struck me about Jennifer's response was the matter-of-fact way in which she referred to her former student's aversion; it was just one thing about him, of the multitude of qualities that made him who he was.

Fast-forward to May of 2006. Caleb has been a member of the inaugural pre-K class at the Little School of Hillsborough since September. It's difficult to put into words just how much joy this year has brought, and just how magical the Little School is—but I will try.

When we arrived at school one day last week, some friends, already on the playground, spied him as he crossed the parking lot. "Caleb!" they yelled, and then started a rhythmic chant: "Ca-leb! Ca-leb! Ca-leb!" He was greeted at the door by one of his best friends, Eli, who hugged him. After a moment, Eli said, "Thanks, Caleb," and Caleb responded, "Thanks, Eli!" They had thanked each other for the hug. Then they ran off to the playground together, as I watched. I hear about or see such lovely moments often. On another morning,

Caleb brought his favorite James Taylor CD to school, and his teacher put on the song "You've Got a Friend." Caleb sang the song, and then all the kids gave each other hugs.

Eli is one of Caleb's lunch buddies also. (The students all eat in their classroom, and the same groups eat lunch together every day, at the same tables.) One of Caleb's challenges is trying new foods; we've been working on helping him overcome this fear all year. So each day at lunch, he has to try one of the lunch foods the Little School provides, in addition to the lunch I pack him from home. At first, this was traumatic, but it's gotten easier and easier. When he is successful, his lunch buddies all say things like "Great job!" and "I'm so proud of you!" Sometimes they give him the thumbs-up sign, or sometimes they give him a hug. This is not for eating brussels sprouts, mind you—this is for taking a bite of an apple, or of pizza, or some macaroni and cheese. Caleb beams with pride in the glow of his friends' enthusiasm for these daily triumphs. He then runs to share the latest news with Christa in the school office. "Guess what!" he announces. "I ate a mango!" Christa will then sometimes bestow upon him a very special treat: He gets to go out to her car and turn on the wipers, or maybe even turn on the radio or open the sun roof. (Caleb has a thing about wipers; he loves them. We're not one hundred percent sure why, but we think he likes the sound they make. He's a sound connoisseur.) The fact that the school's director is taking him into her car to turn on the wipers for eating some fruit, and the fact that his peers are cheering him on, as opposed to making fun of him for being "weird," is indicative of the school's ethos.

Once, the kids were doing an art project that involved squirting water dyed with food coloring from a medicine or eyedropper. Caleb was having none of it. He used to be very unnerved by things that squirt or spray, I think because he was afraid that something that felt horrible would somehow end up on his skin. He watched the project for a long time, steadfastly refusing to go near it. Then he worked up to just touching the dropper—not holding it. Then he was able to hold it, and even squirt it, but only if it contained clear water. At last, after a while, he did the whole shebang—food coloring and all. Christa told me she wished they had videotaped the entire process; it was so wonderful to watch the stages of him working through it. She was as proud of him as she related this story as I would have been. Later, when I told Emily this story, she said, "You know, that's how they are with *all* the kids, not just Caleb."

At the Little School, Caleb is not "separate" or "other"; he is a fully integrated and valued member of the community. I don't think anyone in Caleb's class knows that Caleb is "different." They know that some things are hard for him, so they help him. And he helps others. Most important, he's learning how to join games, take turns, play by the rules, and how to work out things, like sharing bikes or toys, not to mention engage in all kinds of conversations about everything under the sun.

When we got to school this morning, as we crossed the lot, Caleb said, "My friends are waiting for me." This is the same boy who was not eligible, we were told, for any other class but the self-contained autism room, because he could engage only in parallel play. Had we acquiesced to the school district's plans for him, I am convinced irreparable harm would have been done. How is a kid with a language delay and a communications disorder supposed to learn social interaction if his only classmates also have language delays and communication disorders? In Caleb's case, the appropriate environment was the key that unlocked his spirit—the one we always knew was inside him. Now it has taken flight.

The Team Approach

Dawn Mazzeo

Dawn Mazzeo is the mother of Noah, a nine-year-old boy who has been diagnosed with PDD-NOS (high-functioning autism), ADHD, a mood-anxiety disorder, and a tic disorder. She lives in Brooklyn, New York.

For me, hell always began the moment Noah stepped off the school bus. We had moved him from public school to Summit, a private school specializing in bright children with social delay, where there were only eight children (and three teachers) in a classroom. At the time, I thought maybe the fact that he had a long bus ride home on the school's minibus, which pulled up right outside our home every morning and afternoon, set him off. He would literally rage and rage from the time he walked through the door until he fell asleep at night; sometimes he would fall asleep midrage. My younger daughter, Rosie, coped with the madness by escaping to her room to play with her dolls. It wasn't as easy for me: I handled each day the best I could—planning quiet activities for Noah like card games or playing with Play-Doh, trying to reward good behavior and continually tweaking his medication with his doctor to try to take the edge off his irritability.

If something unpredictable or frustrating happened during playtime—if he couldn't form a particular shape with his Play-Doh or if I won a round of cards (usually by accident)—he would scream and cry and run back and forth through the hallways of our apartment. I would try to reassure him by quickly reshaping the dough or offering to play again, but he would not be calmed. He'd work himself into hysterics and would just repeat the wrongdoing over and over again: "I lost! I lost! I lost! I don't want to play again! I will lose again! I will lose again! I always lose! Why did you make me play that stupid game? WHY DID YOU MAKE ME PLAY IT, MOMMY?"

If Rosie should happen in on this episode, he would scream, "MIND YOUR OWN BUSINESS, ROSIE! Stay away from me! Get away! Mommy, make her get away from me!" Poor Rosie would either just stand there, dumbstruck, or she would start to cry.

When Noah would finally stop running through the house, I would try to hold each of his shoulders in one of my hands, trying to reach him and quiet his out-of-control body and voice. Sometimes, upon feeling my touch, he would throw himself down, screaming, "You pushed me! You hurt me!" I would then run around the apartment, closing all the windows. I was terrified someone was going to call the police.

Stressful? Maddening? Unfair? It was all of those things, but when my husband and I considered hospitalizing Noah, I couldn't do it. The idea terrified me: I couldn't imagine a place that would be good enough for my boy.

And, despite all the white-knuckle days, I did not want to be separated from my son. He was only six. So, unproductive as it was, we just kept on doing what we were doing and bearing it. I was perpetually exhausted. When my husband, Michael, came home from work, I could barely speak. He would walk into our bedroom, and I would be sitting in the dark watching television. The kids would be asleep, and I'd be catatonic.

At about the same time, I started to uncontrollably shake during Noah's tantrums. When I told our therapist, Dr. Evans, about this, she concluded that the prolonged stress was affecting my nervous system. She suggested I go on antianxiety medication, and I did. The shaking soon stopped.

Then one day she called to check on me, and she could hear

Noah raging in the background. She said she thought that, although he had been diagnosed earlier as bipolar, his tantrums sounded autistic. She suggested we have him rediagnosed.

Four weeks later, Noah was admitted to a pediatric psychiatric ward at Stony Brook University Hospital, in Stony Brook, New York, two hours away from our home. He spent a total of six weeks on the ward, where they took him off all of his medications. I stayed in Stony Brook during this time while my husband and daughter remained in Brooklyn, so Rosie could go to school and Michael could work.

The diagnosis he was given by the Stony Brook team was pervasive developmental delay (PDD), which meant he had delays across the board—fine and gross motor, social, emotional, and learning. Yet, his tests also confirmed that Noah was an extremely bright child.

We brought him home full of hope—now we could get down to the business of helping him get better. Or so we thought. Even with a revised diagnosis, new medication, and a mother's helper, having Noah at home was mind-blowingly tough. It took everything I had left to get through each day.

The drama was taking its toll on my husband and daughter. Noah was destroying Rosie's self-esteem and sense of well-being. A day did not go by in which, despite our best efforts to restrain him, he did not get up in her face and berate her. Noah was obsessive-compulsive about lining up his toys in rows. If Rosie wandered into his room, picked up a Pokémon character, and put it back in the "wrong" place, he went ballistic, screaming, "You idiot! You idiot! Don't you know that is not where it goes!! MOM, GET HER OUT OF HERE! GET OUT ROSIE! G-E-T O-U-T!!!!!!" I could see her eyes flicker with remorse and fear. Her sense of herself was eroding before my eyes, and it broke my heart. And yet, I had a sick child, and that broke my heart even more.

Then came a Saturday in December of 2003, when Noah was still six—the day that changed our lives forever. It was unusual for us to have a Saturday appointment with Dr. Evans, but we did—because Noah was having a *very* tough weekend. She asked us to come in as a family. Just minutes after the appointment got under way, Noah started to explode. Dr. Evans peered over her bright red glasses and said she wanted to talk to my husband and me "in private." The expression on her face was stone-cold serious. She said, "We have been working together for a year now, and we are nowhere close to where we need to be. It is time to discuss another option. I am afraid if Noah stays in the household, the damage to Rosie will be irreparable. The two of you look like you are falling apart at the seams. Believe me when I say that being this out of control is not good for Noah."

I had to know what this "other option" was—immediately—so I could get started doing it. Noah had tried every medicine in the book. I had installed a sensory integration gym in my house, tried herbal remedies, as well as short-term diagnostic hospitalization for him. I even brushed Noah with a special plastic brush the occupational therapist had given me, every night, to help organize his nervous system and make him less sensitive to touch and hopefully less irritable. What, I wanted to know, was this "other option"? I felt like I was in search of the Holy Grail, only moments away from finally touching it.

"Residential placement," Dr. Evans said. "In other words, a therapeutic school and living environment where trained specialists can address his needs on a deeper, more intensive level. This will allow you and your family some time to heal and regroup as well, without Noah in the house."

I was stunned. Send my baby, my firstborn child, somewhere to live other than with *me*? I still couldn't stomach the idea. I felt like a failure as a mother: I couldn't make him better.

And yet, at that point, I also realized that his problems were bigger than me, and so I faced the fact that we needed expert help—not from a hospital, but from a school and living situation with a highly trained staff who were *always* there to instruct Noah as to how to communicate appropriately with others, without the distraction of having to do laundry or cook dinner or care for a younger sibling.

My husband and I were adamant about not sending him to a school we could not drive to, so we chose the Andrus Children's Center in Yonkers, New York, which is forty-five minutes from our home.

On a sunny January day, my husband, Noah, and I visited the school, toured the beautiful grounds, and saw the boys' cottage. When the head of admissions extended her hand for Noah to shake and he punched it, I thought we were doomed. She told Noah in no uncertain terms, "That behavior is not allowed here. Do you need to take a walk with your mother and calm down, and then come back to speak with me?"

"Yes, that's a good idea," I replied. Noah just frowned ferociously. He knew this was a boarding school, and he did not like the idea of it one bit. After walking the grounds for a few minutes, we found ourselves under the shade of an apple tree. "Okay, here's the deal," I said. "You can go in there and be yourself and speak with her, and when we leave, pick out a new toy dinosaur at the toy store—*or* you can continue to act inappropriately and sit in your room until bedtime once we get home." As it was only eleven in the morning, he chose to go in and speak with the head of admissions.

During their chat, he got frustrated and angry at times, but did manage to share that he liked drawing (he is a talented artist) and playing with Pokémon characters. He revealed that he had an enormous Pokémon collection, and she told him that she knew some of the names of various Pokémon, like Pikachu and Ash. She would say a name, and he would recite the attacks that the character had committed in battle; they conversed like this for a while, Noah enthusiastically educating her. Overall, we were impressed with the ways in which the people at Andrus acted toward Noah: kind and encouraging, but firm. Thankfully, he was accepted. I hugged him when we found out and told him that he was not alone, that there were other children at Andrus just like him who needed help, and that the people who worked there wanted to help him.

At Andrus, he lives in a cottage with sixteen other boys. They are basically smart, delightful kids who no one can live with for various reasons. To look upon these children, you would just see sweet kids. Then something happens, and they're not just sweet kids anymore.

Noah receives reinforcement for his behavior twenty-four hours a day, seven days a week. At Summit, he could not incorporate what he learned at school into his behavior at home. He experienced himself as "two Noahs": a good Noah at school and an out-of-control Noah at home. It was this "splitting" that convinced the board of education to pay for Noah's stay at Andrus—the cost runs in the neighborhood of one hundred thousand dollars per year.

When Noah becomes explosive, his teachers, the staff in the cottage, and his social worker, Jon Kleinman, work closely with him to help him soothe himself. What has become clear during the last eighteen months is that Noah does have some very serious communication (language processing) issues. However, my husband, as it turns out, is very good at understanding and communicating with Noah. I never would have known this if Noah did not go to Andrus: When Noah lived at home, my husband was never home. He just couldn't take it.

Noah comes home every other weekend and spends long holiday breaks with us, too. If his behavior is out of control, he gets a warning from us. If, after the third warning, he has not pulled it together, we take him back to Andrus. They are always available. And because, more than anything, Noah wants to live at home, the stakes are very high for him.

Noah likes Andrus. He has friends and he fits in. When he sees another child out of control, he says, "I used to be like that, and I don't want to be like that anymore." Seeing other children act out of control is a real learning tool for him. Once he said, "Mom, if there were others kids in our house that were my own age, I would hold it together." The group dynamic, not wanting to lose credibility with his peers, serves as a constant incentive for him to hold it together. Noah is one of the highest-functioning kids is his cottage.

I went through a period of real mourning when Noah went to Andrus. Then I realized there was calm in my house again, and I hugged my husband and I hugged my daughter and, over time, we reconnected with one another. Noah is learning how to be a *member* of our family instead of the *main focus* of our family. Once we saw the progress he was making, we knew we had made the right decision.

Most children stay at Andrus for two years. Noah has been there a year and a half, and I hardly recognize him. His main goal is to manage his emotions. My husband and I see Jon Kleinman every other week, and, lately, Noah has been coming to our sessions. He can now take responsibility for the ways in which he used to act at home. He is learning how to change. His psychiatrist says he was simply born with a very rigid, inflexible temperament. She has not changed his meds. My family has a normal life during the week, and on the weekends we give Noah his lab work, so to speak—his hands-on practice of functioning within his family.

Rosie is thriving. She can have friends over at our home now, which she never could before, for fear of Noah getting out of control. She has her issues with growing up this way, of course, and sees a therapist. And she has some residual anger toward how Noah treated her in the past, which we are trying to get her to work through in therapy. Now that she is older, she can better express herself verbally and better understand what her brother's limitations are.

As Noah enters puberty, we will keep a close eye on him. We

hope he comes home to live with us soon but do not want to push him too hard. When his teachers, the cottage staff, his social worker, and my husband, daughter, and I all think he is ready, he will move back and attend Andrus as a day student. Our family and his teachers and therapists at Andrus are a team. I see the light at the end of a very dark, very long tunnel. Noah is going to be well.

Trust Your Instincts

Stephanie Ruby

Stephanie Ruby is the mother of Deuce, who is six and in the process of being diagnosed with a variety of disorders—Asperger's syndrome, ADHD, and social anxiety and sensory integration disorders. She and her family live in West Manchester, Ohio.

When my son, Deuce, was three years old, my husband, Shawn, and I decided that enrolling him in preschool would be a good way for him to make friends and would help to prepare him for kindergarten. Although he had been a difficult baby, Deuce spoke extremely early, talking in sentences by the time he was a year old. At sixteen months, he could name complex shapes, way beyond the normal "square, circle, triangle" that most babies could identify.

But Deuce *hated* preschool. One day, he came home distraught over his crayons. It took me a while to figure out exactly what he was saying through all the sobbing, but I eventually understood that his teacher had dumped all the crayons from the children's boxes (each child had brought their own school box and supplies at the beginning of the year) into the middle of the table, and that during the cleanup process he ended up with "wrong" crayons in his box. No other child cared, but he couldn't get past it. It seemed so insignificant—why did he focus on things that didn't matter? After sending Deuce to this school for less than a month, we decided to pull him out. He begged every morning to stay home; he wasn't making friends, and he already knew how to count to one hundred, and knew the names of all the shapes and colors, and anything else he needed to know to be ready for elementary school.

Seeing the degree to which Deuce just, honestly, could not handle school made us realize that he would probably do best if he were educated at home—and so I learned as much as I could about homeschooling, and dove right in. Deuce is six now, and I have been homeschooling him for the past three years; our plan is to homeschool him through high school. Luckily for us, Deuce is so bright that most lessons have come easily for him.

Being at home for most of the day makes it easy for Deuce to have control over his environment. There are no strange smells or overly loud noises (besides his little brother), or school lunches with unfamiliar textures, or uncomfortable, hard chairs. When he is feeling like he needs a sensory break, he takes it. He has proven to us that, as long as he feels like he has some measure of control over what goes on during his day, he can thrive.

Deuce does best when given frequent breaks and when he has a say in how the day is going to progress. Every morning, he goes to our refrigerator and grabs his "schedule magnets" (a homemade set of magnets with pictures of all his daily activities, such as schoolwork, chores, meals, and snacks) off of the side, and then puts them in the order he wishes the day to proceed. He schedules his own breaks and decides which subjects he feels up to doing, when he feels up to it. After that, we just follow the schedule, moving each magnet to the "done" side of the refrigerator as a task is completed. Bad days mean that we won't get as much schoolwork done, but we do get to practice appropriate emotional responses to stress.

Because Deuce spends most of his time with Shawn and me, we can model appropriate social behaviors for him, so that as he grows, he has the socialization skills necessary to interact appropriately. I believe that if it weren't for homeschooling, he would have many more issues. These issues could be anything from a lower tolerance for noise to dealing with the stress that comes from being forced to interact with so many children for seven hours a day.

Homeschooling was also a turning point in discovering what may be wrong with him. One evening in July 2005, I was on the Internet talking to other homeschoolers about ways to help Deuce focus more during school. After describing some of his behaviors, another mom suggested that his behavior sounded similar to that of her son who had Asperger's syndrome. I had never heard of this before, so I immediately began researching it on the Web and checking out books on it from the library. As I read, I felt so many things, from amazement that these books were describing my son, who never "fit" anywhere, to relief upon finding that I wasn't a bad parent. I was also quite upset, of course, to learn that my son had issues that couldn't be solved with simple discipline. And then dread set in, as I wondered how Deuce would take the news if in fact he was diagnosed with Asperger's syndrome.

Two years ago, we switched pediatricians because we were having trouble getting our former pediatrician to take my concerns over Deuce's quirks seriously. When we brought up the possibility of Asperger's with his new doctor, however, she listened. We then got the referral we needed to see a developmental pediatrician, to evaluate Deuce. Since then, he has been through extensive testing to try to clarify what is going on with him, and we are finally getting answers. We have recently gotten the official diagnoses that Deuce has Asperger's sydrome, sensory integration disorder (SID), and attention deficit hyperactivity disorder (ADHD). We are still waiting to find out if he also has central auditory processing disorder (CAPD).

Had it not been for our decision to homeschool Deuce, I may not have gotten to know my son so intimately, and may not have come across the information about Asperger's online. Deuce could have continued to suffer in school unnecessarily. Instead, he is thriving.

SECTION 5

To Medicate or Not to Medicate

L et me begin by stating that *I am not for or against using medication to treat psychiatric illness.* Taking medication—or, even more tricky, deciding whether to give it to your child—is a private, complicated, harrowing decision. As you will see in this section, it can be the scariest, and sometimes the best, choice you can make for a child in pain.

What interested me most about the contributions I read for this book was not that the majority of the parents ultimately chose to put their child on medication (which is true), but how each parent came to his or her decision. They were thoughtful. They were cautious. And I found this very admirable. Resisting the urge to want to find a "magic pill" (or what we call in my house a PCP—perfect child pill) can be difficult when you're at your wit's end. Like my husband and me, many of the parents in this section had life-altering, epic arguments with each other and near-catastrophes with their kids leading up to their decision to medicate. They often felt worn down, worried, and tired to the bone. The closer they got to insanity, the more each parent craved normalcy. Medication offered hope—and a chance of success.

Many parents in this book don't hide the fact that, as their children's conditions worsened, they turned to medication for *themselves*. When her son, Matt, began to act out, Veronica, a mom from Queens, New York, developed panic attacks. "After a long time of thinking I was going crazy, I finally went to a doctor," she writes. "The antianxiety medication the doctor prescribed to me does help." While some people try to simply wait out the symptoms of mental illness, like Veronica, others become extremely proactive and seek out every possible alternative before they will accept a prescription, for themselves or for their kids. Leigh Anne Wilson of Plainfield, Illinois, writes: "Three years, dozens of occupational therapy sessions, parenting classes, allergy tests, new diet regimes, mercury testing, eye examinations, and every last dime of our money later, we ended up before a group of psychiatrists at Children's Memorial Hospital in Chicago. They handed us a prescription for Ritalin."

One important truth I observed in collecting these stories is that medicating is more an art than a science—and each parent, including my husband and me, simply had to trust his or her gut when making their decision. Our collective family gut said this: My son was battling something in his body. His brain was making him extremely anxious, depressed, and nervous. The upshot: He couldn't enjoy being a kid because he was sick. We began thinking of Toby's problems as part of a disease and not some odd form of behavioral manipulation. That's how we came to be okay with the idea of giving him Prozac. Of course, post-meds, some things stayed the same: He was still scared of water (a fear that just recently went away). He was furious, initially, about the idea of not being able to sleep in our bed each night. And he was insanely jealous of his sister. But the antidepressants lessened the severity of his responses. That changed our lives for the better.

But let me back up and make this clear: The moment I handed my child a pill and watched him swallow it while he was watching Nickelodeon and drinking out of a sippy cup was frightening. I ran to the bathroom and cried after I did it the first time. These days knowing my son is on medication gets easier to stomach, for one reason: I can see how far he's come. I have come to realize that giving him a daily dose every morning makes sense.

In the midst of finishing this section of the book, I began to worry that I had not included the stories of any parents who had *turned down* medication. On a hunt for these essays, I began to call back contributors whose pieces I had not included in the final draft of the collection for one reason or another, to see if any of them had backed off of medication or found effective alternative treatments—melatonin and omega-3 fatty acids and biofeedback and so forth—since we last spoke. Had their reality changed? How did they feel about medication now? Many who were initially opposed to medication reported that, in the end, they decided to give it a try. One mom explained, "We know my son is bipolar, and although we tried everything for the last year, we are starting medication on Monday." Others, particularly those on the autistic spectrum, told me they *had* used alternative therapies, and were pleased with how helpful they seemed, but were more open-minded about medication than ever before. Why? I asked each parent. One said: "I know these are strong, scary drugs, but if things get really bad, well, we'll try anything we can to get our daughter better." Point taken.

Why We Chose Meds

Leigh Anne Wilson

Leigh Anne Wilson is the mother of Alex, age six, who has been diagnosed with four consecutive disorders: sensory integration disorder, Asperger's syndrome, ADHD, and, finally, pervasive developmental disorder. They live in Plainfield, Illinois.

No bones about it—it's lonely being the parent of a child with behavioral disorders. You feel like nobody else really understands what you're going through—not other parents, not teachers, and sometimes not even doctors. You even think about your own views, back in your child-free, size 6 jean days, and realize that young, skinny you wouldn't have understood, either.

Before Alex and his younger brother, Christopher, were born, I thought I would be the best parent in the world. I thought I was ready to sail forth into parenthood, guided by my carefully honed theories, formed from adolescent criticism of my own mother and a few from television sitcoms. I stood confidently on the dock, watching the sailors haphazardly baling water out of their leaky dinghies. How contemptuous I was of their blind, obvious mistakes! How stupid were their choices! How incapable they were of applying the firm but cool hand that I was sure to do, were I in their shoes. And yet, when it finally came time for me to step into my own boat, not one sailor was surprised to see that foot plunge right through the floor, tipping the boat right over. Nobody was surprised to see how I struggled to keep my head above the water. Nobody but me, anyway.

The six years of Alex's life can be divided almost evenly into two parts: the first three years, when I thought something was wrong with me, and the next three years, when I still thought something was wrong with me, but I now also thought maybe something was going on with him, too. I spent the first few years of Alex's life trying to get the boy to act right. I couldn't do it. I couldn't get him to stop breaking everything he got his hands on. I couldn't stop him from coloring on the walls. I couldn't get him to use the potty, couldn't get him to quit plugging the bathroom sinks and flooding the upstairs, and, worst of all, I couldn't get him to acknowledge my cries of "No!" even when he was darting toward the street or trying to stick his hand in a roaring fire.

In an attempt to gain some control over our lives, I installed locks on the bathroom and bedroom doors and removed the furniture from Alex's room and the playroom. I bought board books he couldn't rip up, and let him use a sippy cup well past his babyhood to prevent him from pouring whatever he was drinking onto the computer keyboard or his own pillow—this was easier than trying to change him. If Alex was warned in advance not to exhibit a particular behavior, it was like handing him an engraved invitation to do exactly that. And everybody—from bag boys at the grocery store to strangers on an airplane—gave me instructions on how to get Alex to comply. Most of the time they wouldn't believe me when I told them their suggestions had already been tried and had bombed. Often I just went along with them because I knew that the quicker I gave in, the quicker it would fail, and the quicker they would wash their hands of us and go away. (Before they'd go, though, they all seemed to be in agreement that raising my child was no problem, as long as they were the ones doing it.)

By the time I was heavily pregnant with Christopher, the looks I was getting from the teachers at Alex's new Montessori preschool were clear: *Two? You can't even handle the one you've got.* He was expelled from Montessori two weeks after the beginning of the fall semester for behavioral issues, and while he was finishing out the year at a lower-rent preschool, his kindly teacher, Miss Nancy, suggested that we have him tested for ADD.

"I've been teaching preschool for twenty-five years," she said, "and he's a textbook case."

We took him to get a professional opinion, the first of the many, many opinions we were to get. Three years, dozens of occupational therapy sessions, parenting classes, allergy tests, new diet regimes, mercury testing, eye examinations, adenoid removal, and every last dime of our money later, we ended up sitting before a group of psychiatrists at Children's Memorial Hospital in Chicago. They handed us a prescription for Ritalin. The decision to medicate was not made without a certain amount of crow-eating, as my husband and I both had long believed that too many little boys were on Ritalin when all they really needed was more exercise. But here we were at long last, clutching the last straw. We had taken the boys out to lunch at RJ Grunts, a family-friendly restaurant across the street from the Lincoln Park Zoo, and were quietly talking about Ritalin. I was willing to try it, my husband less so. As we sat, Alex leaped up, ran to the salad bar, and started scooping up black olives with the serving spoon and shoving the spoon in his mouth. It was as if he did not even hear us yelling at him, first to come back, then to stop, STOP! He would not stop shoveling olives into his maw until my husband finally reached him and jerked him away, prying his fingers from around the spoon. It might have been funny if it wasn't so humiliating. Or if we hadn't bankrupted ourselves trying every method possible to get him to cease exactly that kind of behavior, short of wrapping him up in duct tape or lobotomizing him. (Oh, or taking Ritalin.) My husband yanked Alex back to the table and scolded him. Alex rolled his eyes around in his head, flapped his hands, and replied, inexplicably, "Mrs. Puff, I do have an antenna under my hat!" I'd never seen such a look of resignation on my husband's face before.

"Okay," he said softly. "We'll try the Ritalin."

The first day Alex took his recommended dose of two pills, he lay immobile on the couch literally all day long, completely dragged down and crankier than I'd ever seen him. The psychiatrist recommended we cut his dosage in half. On the half dose, he drew a picture of a house with himself, Christopher, Mommy, and Daddy all standing outside. The sun was yellow, the grass was green, the door was white, and all the happy stick figures, three bald and one with a brown ponytail, were waving. Before the Ritalin, his drawings had almost always been feverish monochromatic purple or black scrawls, sweaty with energy but no apparent thought behind them. The following week he began reading. The week after that he brought home a sheet of arithmetic he had completed. All the answers were correct. The week after that he brought home a friend, who played trains with him all afternoon.

And when we had our first parent-teacher conference, his teacher told us that when Alex was called out of her class for therapy, she challenged the instructor over it.

"I couldn't believe he needed special classes," she told us. "He's one of my best students."

For six years I've cried over my inability to make an impact on Alex, and over my mistakes, both real and imaginary. I've broken down over people telling me all the things I've done wrong, and over all the useless times I yelled at him or spoke harshly to him about his compulsive behavior. I cried two weeks after a feature about One Good Thing—the blog I write to keep a record of my children's lives in lieu of scrapbooking—was published in the *Chicago Tribune*, when I discovered that we were featured on a "child free" Internet forum as proof for the need for forced sterilization. And, of course, I've cried over not being able to do what mothers are supposed to do: make everything better. But I wasn't used to crying like I did when I heard his teacher tell us what a pleasure it was to have him in her class.

Comedian Caroline Rhea once joked that instead of saying, "Screw you!" like New Yorkers do, Southern people instead say, "Bless your heart." ("You think all Southerners are illiterate? Well, bless your heart, no!") I've been bearing that particular bit of standup in mind, now that the newest crop of criticisms have started to arrive from those who don't approve of Ritalin or those who think, like I used to think, it's just a crutch for lazy parents. After six years of watching my baby get rejected by peers as he whirled and shrieked around them, after watching him get expelled from school and listening to the parents of his classmates express relief to my face that he was away from their children, Alex deserves this first taste of success. And it looks like it's going to be Ritalin that gives it to him after all. And if you don't approve of that, well, bless your heart.

What Worked for Us

Harriet Brown

Harriet Brown is a journalist and the mother of Soleil, age eleven, who has panic disorder and childhood depression. She is the editor of Mr. Wrong: Real-Life Stories About the Men We Used to Love, *and the author of* The Good-Bye Window. *She and her family live in Madison, Wisconsin.*

I've had panic disorder ever since I was about eight years old. I've gone through periods of frequent panic attacks that made ordinary life painful and that led me to become phobic about many things—elevators, heights, being alone—in my teens and early twenties. Despite my own experience, however, it took me months to figure out that my eight-year-old daughter, Soleil, was having panic attacks.

After being treated in the hospital for Kawasaki's syndrome—a rare and potentially lethal disease—Soleil recovered physically but seemed changed in other ways. She started throwing temper tantrums—the full-body, four-on-the-floor kind my husband and I hadn't seen since she was three. She also developed severe anxiety around thunderstorms, and the slightest possibility of a tornado in our Midwestern city sent her into paroxysms of what looked like rage. She'd always been out there, emotionally, but before her illness, I could read her moods, her ups and downs; I could tune in to what she was feeling. These tantrums, though, went way beyond anything I could understand.

The "aha" moment for me came one evening at the Wisconsin State Fair, when she and her twelve-year-old sister got on a ride together—the kind where you stand up against a spinning wall, in the dark, and the floor drops away. I watched them disappear happily into the ride, and I watched the ride start up. Then I watched the ride slow down and stop, the door open, and my daughters stumble out, both of them incandescent with rage.

"She started screaming before the ride even started," hissed the older one, her face scarlet with embarrassment. "I had to yell at them to get someone to open the doors."

I turned to my younger daughter, whose brows were drawn together ominously.

"Were you scared?" I asked.

She stomped her foot and shook her head. "I feel like I'm going to throw up!" she screamed. With those words, something clicked in my brain. I knelt beside her.

"Does your stomach hurt?" I asked. She stomped again, even more furious.

"No!" she yelled. "I feel like I'm going to pass out!"

I got her to look into my eyes, breathe deeply with me. I talked soothingly. After about five minutes she was herself again—not her old bubbly self, but the new post-disease self, the one I hadn't quite recognized. Later that week I found myself telling the pediatrician that, yes, she'd become more withdrawn, her friendships had suffered— even the list of foods she was willing to eat was shrinking. She was pulling in on all fronts, but, until recently, I hadn't seen it. I'd been scanning for fear, not rage.

The pediatrician explained that children with panic disorder and depression often look angry or irritable rather than fearful or sad. He explained the treatment options: Do nothing and hope it goes away after six months or so (which it might); try her on an antidepressant like Prozac; try her on an antidepressant *and* send her to a play therapist. I am a science and medical journalist, and I knew that a combination of medication and therapy generally produces the best results—in theory, with someone else's children. But for my eight-year-old, my baby?

Should we put her on medication that would alter her growing brain, possibly forever? And what about the "black box" warnings about children and antidepressants and suicide? I thought back to my own childhood and adolescence, which had been dominated by panic attacks, episodes of intense fear that often struck at night, when I was trying to go to sleep. I didn't know they were panic attacks, of course; I just thought I was going insane. What if Prozac had been around when I was a kid?

My husband asked the doctor, "What would you do if she were your child?"

The pediatrician didn't hesitate. "I'd treat her," he said. "I'd watch her carefully, but I'd try her on the medication." He wrote us a prescription, which lay on my desk for a week before I screwed up the courage to have it filled. It took another week before I was ready to explain to Soleil that these pills might help the scary feelings she'd been having. She swallowed one willingly every morning, while my husband and I held our breaths, waiting to see what happened.

We didn't wait long. By the third day we could see the change; the muscles in her face looked more relaxed. She smiled more. After a week a neighbor who knew nothing of this called to say that Soleil seemed like her old self again. And she did: There were no more rages. She gradually became more social. She still had panic attacks, but now we could talk about them. She started seeing a therapist. A year later, we tried to wean her off the Prozac. Within three weeks, the tantrums came back. Two days after starting her up again, she was fine.

She's still afraid of thunder and heights, still fears tornadoes. But now she manages her fears, rather than the other way around. She's learned that she doesn't have to be a helpless victim of terror. She's learned that she has power in the world—the power to ask for help and receive it, the power to control her own thoughts and feelings. Next year, when she's twelve, we'll try again to wean her off the medication. If the same thing happens, though, we'll put her back on it without a qualm. My hope is that if we spare her the depression and panic disorder now, maybe they won't become lifelong companions. Maybe they won't shape her life the way they shaped mine.

The way I see it, the risks of not treating her far outweigh the risks of treating her. Whenever I have a moment's doubt, I remember the look on her face as she tumbled out of that ride, and I'm grateful once more that we have the ability to make her whole again.

My Son Is Still Alive

Kimberly

Kimberly is the mother of Derek, age twelve, who has bipolar disorder. They live in Missouri.

My son, Derek, is twelve now, and he is still here with me. I consider that to be a miracle. Experts say he has an 18 to 20 percent chance of taking his own life—given his diagnosis of bipolar disorder—so I feel we have been pretty lucky so far.

I take those statistics very seriously because at eight years old, while on the wrong medication, Derek tried to take his life. He came into the kitchen and proceeded to pull a rope tight around his neck. This incident happened after many doctors and family members tried to convince me that he was normal.

Normal? From day one I knew that my son was different. At six months old, he had to listen to the vacuum running to fall sleep. Even at such a young age, he was never satisfied for long, never calm for long. He never slept for more than a couple of hours at a time. In most of his baby videos he is crying—and when he cried, he had to be rocked so hard in the rocking chair that I felt like I was on an amusement park ride. The terrible twos came like a tsunami. Derek quickly grew big and strong, and he was a powerful force to reckon with when he was told no. In addition, he seemed to be oversensitive to even the smallest things. The toast was too crunchy, the socks were too tight, the television was too loud. We learned both to tiptoe around him and to give in to his every wish, just to keep the house intact.

And I mean that literally. If he wanted something to eat, he would scream at the top of his lungs if I couldn't give it to him immediately. . He would bang around on the floor or throw things for just about any—or no—reason. Before having children, I had worked in preschools with toddlers for three years. But I had never seen a force like my son at this age. Everyday living was like walking through a minefield.

At the same time, on his good days, he was very funny and extremely smart. And as he has gotten older and more stable, he can be very loving, considerate, helpful, and insightful beyond his years. Despite his behavior issues, he has many positive qualities that wax and wane as symptoms come and go.

When Derek was two and his older sister, Lacey, was six, their father, Ken, and I separated. Five years later, Ken died in a motorcycle accident. The loss was unbearable for the children, and it was difficult for me, too, as Ken and I were still on amicable terms. It was right before his death that Ken realized that Derek did indeed need to be seen by mental health professionals. This was after many major battles between us. For a long time he didn't believe anything was wrong with *his* boy.

After Derek's suicide attempt—which happened about a year after his father's death—and subsequent diagnosis of having early-onset childhood bipolar disorder, I sunk into a grief I could have never imagined. I'll admit I had a pretty shaky childhood and early adulthood, but I had never felt grief like this. Alone with my feelings most of the time, I often found myself stuck on the question, *Why us?* The only thing that seemed to help my state of mind was educating myself about Derek's disease. The more I knew, the more I could explain his condition to my family and friends—and the more they understood, the more they could, ideally, support me. Like Ken, many of the people close to us were initially dismissive of the idea that something could be psychologically wrong him.

Every day, I would research bipolar disorder on the Internet, and print out anything I thought might help friends and family gain a better understanding of what Derek and I were going through. Having a diagnostic "phrase" we could use to talk about my son—after so many years of not knowing *how* to explain what was going on with him—was helpful. One by one, most of our friends and family came around, after they dealt with their own feelings of denial.

Still, having a child with this disorder doesn't rally people together like with other, strictly physical diseases. Even after I explained Derek's disease to friends and family members, many asked if he would outgrow it; they just didn't understand that this was a lifelong illness.

Feeling so alone, I began visiting a Web site recommended in a book I'd read on bipolar children—the site for the Child and Adolescent Bipolar Foundation (CABF), www.bpkids.org. I soon began logging on to this site day and night, asking other parents like me literally hundreds of questions on its chat and message boards. These parents—whom I had never met before in person—were kind and empathetic, and they gave me invaluable insight into my son's behavior. Thanks to their advice, for instance, I got counseling for my daughter, who, despite the fact that she was older, bore much of the abuse from my son.

Reading the posts on the site, I felt lucky that Derek didn't hallucinate, jump through windows, or out of cars. I read about kids on the wrong medications—kids who cut their pets with steak knives because they were manic and depressed at the same time. I began to understand what is called "mixed states"—in which sadness, grandiosity, and irritability all came together. Now I understood why my son would flip from sad to mad to glad in less than an hour—several times per day!

I was gradually beginning to understand my son's mind—yet his doctors and I were still at a loss to find the right mix of medication for him. It took four long years for doctors to finally get it right, and he missed a good chunk of third and fourth grade due to hospital visits and side effects. In writing this essay, I reviewed Derek's medication history, and I was stunned. In five years he has been on nineteen different medications, in different combinations and different dosages. It's so extremely scary to put your child on meds in the first place, and then have to change them, raise the dose, and still find no "right" fit for so many years—it was almost too much.

And yet, it's even scarier to have to send your child to a children's psychiatric hospital. Each time my son was admitted, his clothes and shoes were taken away, and he was forced to wear what the facility provided. His other possessions had to be "earned back" over the next forty-eight hours, for "safety reasons." He was not allowed to call home. On one occasion, he was locked in a padded room for refusing to write several pages about his relationship with me during a therapy session. He hates writing! Sometimes, I look back and I don't know how we got through it. It's now been four years since his last hospitalization, yet he still talks about incidents that took place while he was admitted—sad moments, terrifying moments. And he knows that if he doesn't take his lithium (the medication they eventually put him on), he could end up going back. I've pounded this into his head since he started lithium at age nine, and will continue to do so— despite the pain and conflict doing so causes within me.

Derek has lost a "normal" childhood. At twelve years old, he doesn't have many friends. His anxiety keeps him from places like Disney World and even Boy Scout overnights. He can be terrified of one escalator but not the next. He's hesitant to climb trees, ride on boats—all the things he should be enjoying.

After what we experienced, I felt compelled to help other parents. After one of his hospital visits, I stood out in the parking lot after sundown and passed out flyers that I had typed up that week, advertising the CABF Web site that had helped me so much. As I handed the flyers to parents like me, I saw a look of utter defeat, exhaustion, fear, and hopelessness in their faces. It was like looking in a mirror. I soon found that helping others in this way was far more therapeutic and uplifting than sitting around asking, *Why us?*

A few years ago, I founded a local support group so that I could meet with other parents who, like me, were living on Planet Bipolar. Until then, there had been no such support group here in the Kansas City metropolitan area. Talking on the computer was great, but I needed more. So I posted on the CABF Web site and hung flyers at our psychiatrist's office. One by one, parents called or e-mailed, knowing they were reaching out to someone who understood their world. For the first few meetings, only two or three moms showed up, then some dads joined us, then some siblings. For two years, we met over dinner, sharing our joys and sorrows. Meetings were the one public place I could say, "My son punched a hole in the wall when I asked him to brush his teeth today" and nobody would flinch or roll their eyes. *Been there, done that* was their attitude—nothing could shock them. They also lived in a war zone. When your child threatens the safety of parents, siblings, neighbors, and pets, it's not something you can always talk so openly about. Here, in our anything-goes support group, I felt like I was finally being proactive. I was helping those who were coming up behind us.

At the time of this writing, Derek is able to live at home, get by in school, and find happiness in the little stuff. When he laughs out loud it is like a breath of fresh air in our house. These days, when he's teary-eyed, it's usually only for moments, not hours or days.

Lithium has saved his life. And yet, I still worry about the effects it may have on his body. I worry about his being overweight, a common side effect of the medication. I worry about the damage the medication may be doing to his kidneys, another known problem with lithium. Will his organs be okay in thirty years?

When I'm not worried about his body, I worry about his mind. Even on medication he is stable, but not "normal" like his peers at school. I worry about his future: Will he marry? Will he be able to finish high school? Get a good job? Will his high intelligence factor into his future, or will it be buried with emotional problems? Will he be able to maintain his great sense of humor and creativity?

I try to give Derek hope by telling him about astronauts, artists, and writers who have all suffered with manic depression. My son is off to middle school next year. It's easy to accommodate a kid in a wheelchair; not so easy to accommodate a child who looks normal but has an "invisible wheelchair." But that's mental illness. For my part, I will continue to remind him of how far he's come, and that I will always be here for him.

Keep This in Mind

Rick Porter

Rick* is the father of S, who is twenty-six years old and who was diagnosed with ADD at sixteen. He lives in Oregon.

I was a part-time dad—a divorce separated me from my daughters by about eighty miles while they were in elementary school. I didn't witness the screaming fights my elder daughter, who I'll call S, had with her mom and stepdad, although when the girls visited me, her younger sister often told me about S's aggressive behavior. And I noticed immediately how disruptive S could be on weekends at my home. Even simple things, like sending both girls out into the backyard to rake leaves, quickly turned into a disaster. I remember one weekend, when the girls were thirteen and ten, and I gave them this task. I figured it would take two determined workers about an hour to do the entire job. As it turned out, I had one determined worker, my youngest—and one who was completely and utterly distracted.

I'd glance out the window in the midst of my own chores, and during that hour, this is what I saw: S fetched gloves, went to the bathroom, changed gloves, changed rakes, played with the dog, fetched the boom box, changed tapes several times, got several glasses of water, changed shoes, changed coats, and tormented her sister, who raked the entire time.

I spent a lot of time observing my girls—and I would occasionally

*Names have been changed.

wonder whether it was personality differences that caused the problems or whether there was something more serious going on with S. But pushing for medication and therapy? I was so caught up in how to spend quality time with my girls that big-picture worries took a backseat to getting through the days I was with them.

I think we all knew something wasn't right from the time S was young, but divorce and distance made it difficult for me to tackle the problem. It was too easy for me to not deal with her abysmal grades. Still laboring under guilt from the divorce, I rationalized: What could I do with so little actual contact? Her mom implemented a carrot-and-stick approach—first withholding privileges, then cajoling, then punishing, with occasional success but mostly frustration.

On good days, S could just as easily be a joy. She loved to read and talk about books. She shared her parents' goofy sense of humor. And she was almost always optimistic about herself, her abilities, and her future. It didn't ever seem to occur to her that setbacks were permanent.

So it was easy for me to focus on the positives: She had an impressive vocabulary, a high IQ, and she could read long before she started school. But her grades never measured up. Neither did her classroom behavior. Looking back, I realize she had all the stereotypical traits of attention deficit disorder—fidgety, disruptive, forgetful. She didn't finish homework assignments. She had trouble getting along with peers and teachers. She was hyperemotional—joyful one moment, in tears the next. Her failures were always somebody else's fault: This teacher didn't like her, the classroom was too noisy or too quiet, the other kids made fun of her. . . .

In a last-ditch attempt to improve her school performance, her mom and stepdad gave in to her pleas to attend an "alternative" middle school. There students chose their classes and were on the honor system, coming and going from the open campus at will, nobody taking roll or riding herd. While S loved the freedom, she totally failed the honor system, regularly skipping class to smoke in a nearby park, not completing assignments, getting further and further behind. The school told her it wasn't working out, and she had to start high school back at a traditional school.

That year, when she was fifteen, we did take her to a children's clinic. A physician and a psychologist examined and tested her. After speaking with me, her mother, and her stepdad, the doctor diagnosed my daughter with ADD. She got a prescription for Ritalin and weekly counseling for a few months at the clinic; her mom tried consistent positive reinforcement of good behavior.

She told us that she liked the feeling the medication gave her of being able to focus and complete projects. It was a huge relief for everyone involved—but boy, did I feel guilty. How much easier might her childhood have been if we had started her on medication sooner? To this day, I very much regret not getting her help earlier. It's only conjecture—and maybe it's my guilt speaking—but I think that earlier intervention might have helped her lay a better foundation for herself. I regret not realizing that a learning disability, mental illness, or psychological disorder is not the parents' fault, or the fault of a divorce. I regret not realizing earlier that it is my responsibility to do everything I can for my daughter.

It pained me to watch S struggle, even when we did finally put her on medication. Always rail-thin and a poor eater, she found the drugs hurt her stomach and ruined her appetite. And she grew to hate the way they sometimes alienated her from her own emotions. She stopped taking the pills sometime in her senior year, just three years after going on them.

Before long, her old ways returned. She lost expensive retainers and glasses at school, and within a few weeks of getting her driver's license, she'd had three fender benders. She graduated, but barely. An attempt at attending a four-year university (she'd always wanted to be a teacher) ended in failure in the middle of her second year.

Her mother and I pulled the plug on her funds when, semester after semester, she got Cs, Ds, Fs, and incompletes.

Nearly a decade later, after bouncing aimlessly from one low-wage job and unstable living situation to another, she finally seems to be gaining some stability. She seems to have found her niche in wholesale telemarketing—it's not the most glamorous of fields, but it pays well, and some employers even offer health benefits. She has been in the same rental house for more than a year and has some simple goals: to purchase a used car, to attend some community college classes. Maybe she's started to grow out of her condition. Or maybe she's just gotten tired of her very shaky lifestyle. Maybe the past few years of heart-wrenching "tough love" helped; when she withdrew from college, her mother and I finally made it clear that she was on her own and would have to take responsibility for her actions, whether they stemmed from her illness or not

Much to our relief, she is coming around. And she continues to amaze me with her positive outlook and resilience. Still, looking back, I can't help but believe that early treatment might have saved us all a lot of heartache and frustration.

A Different Boy

Veronica

Veronica is the mother of Matt,* age twenty, who was diagnosed with schizophrenia. She and her family live in Queens, New York.

When Matt was seven years old, our lives changed forever. He became a different person—not the little boy who happily went to Catholic school every morning and came home to play peacefully with his two young siblings, Gloria and Ben. He had always been a quiet child. I had no idea that I would soon spend my days managing my son's medication and working with the state to monitor—and hopefully change—his completely erratic behavior.

Here's how our nightmare began: One day, out of the clear blue sky, Matt had a grand mal seizure. His whole body shook, his eyes rolled back, and he began to drool. He lost control of all voluntary and involuntary movement. He had eleven seizures in total that night. Then he went into a coma and stayed unconscious for three days. Doctors explained that Matt had suffered brain damage and that the seizure disorder was going to result in developmental delays and setbacks. He had to learn to walk and talk all over again. He became paranoid. He heard voices. And then he got violent.

In the months after the coma, Matt recovered physically, but his behavior was beyond my control. No matter what medication he was

*Names have been changed.

on, he would act out, run away, shatter windows, and curse, among other things. It seemed no medication could help.

This behavior continued for four years. He went from one school to the next, repeatedly getting expelled for his actions. By this time, he was diagnosed as paranoid schizophrenic and was given Ritalin and Clonapin, an antianxiety medication. After a particularly bad incident where he attacked his sixth-grade teacher in the classroom, his doctors told me it might be best to place Matt out of the home, although they didn't specify in what kind of facility. Not convinced, I begged his doctors to just try to stabilize him on the right meds. I was so sure at the time that he needed to be home with us, in the safety of our one-family home in Queens, New York.

I managed Matt's problems for a total of five years, with the help of the state and the local board of education. The city sent home attendants to help me care for him and my other children. We continued to have to switch schools often because he was constantly misbehaving. Taking Matt's cue, my other son began to act out, too, mimicking the things Matt did, like having tantrums, slamming doors, running away when something wasn't going right. Ben figured, if Matt could do it, why couldn't he? I spent a lot of time explaining to Ben that Matt did what he did because he was sick.

Around that time, I developed panic attacks—and I have them to this day. After a long time of thinking I was going crazy, I went to a doctor. I told him that, from time to time, I get scared for no reason. My heart starts to race. I get tense and feel like I want to escape, but have nowhere to go. I explained how, mostly, this would happen when I was in the car. I would feel like I wanted to just open the door and jump out. The antianxiety medication the doctor prescribed does help, thank God. However, an unnerving side effect of the disorder cropped up: I began to notice that fear of having a panic attack can actually bring on a panic attack, medication or not. I now avoid doing certain things for fear of having a panic attack—particularly driving, since the first time I had a panic attack was when I was in the car.

When he was ten years old, Matt jumped out the second-floor window of our house because I wouldn't let him go outside. We had gone shopping earlier that day with the home attendant, and Matt was being erratic, throwing tantrums. When we got home, he went outside and wrote "Veronica is a bitch" with chalk on the street. I ushered him inside and told him to go take a nap upstairs, but he wanted to go back outside. I told him he had to go to his room. That's when he jumped.

When I saw him lying still on the ground in front of the house, I prayed he hadn't broken his neck. As I was calling 9-1-1, Matt got up from the ground and ran down the block. The police finally found him blocks away. At the hospital, I was surrounded by cops asking all sorts of questions. (They briefly suspected this was a case of child abuse.) When they finally let me see my son, I walked into his room and asked him how he felt. There were doctors and nurses and cops standing all around us.

It was then that I knew I couldn't keep him. That I would not be taking Matt home. After what had happened, I finally accepted that my son needed to be placed in an in-patient facility for at-risk children. In the weeks that followed, social workers helped me place him in appropriate treatment centers throughout New York. First he was placed in Elmhurst Psychiatric Hospital for a thirty-day evaluation. From there, he went to Creedmore Psychiatric Center, where he stayed for a year and a half. Now he is at the Judge Rotenberg Center, a residential behavior-management school, where he has been since 1999. I love the place. I thank God for the care they have given him. With the help of the staff there, Matt has come a long way—and, while finding the right combination of medication has played a large part in this, his progress goes beyond this. He doesn't appear to be hearing voices the way he was before. He's a lot calmer. He's not as paranoid now. Recently, I took him to the Bronx Zoo—he was calm and mature, and he loved it. Years ago, I would never have been able to do this; he would have thought everybody was looking at him.

Now, at age twenty, a new chapter in our life is about to begin. My son is about to age out of the program he is currently in. I don't know what's going to happen next—I worry about how he will do once he graduates from the school that has done so much for him. That will be another adventure to embark on. Wish us good luck.

SECTION 6

Going Public

A wonderful writer I know once described the difference between owning a cat and owning a dog like this: "Having cats is a private thing—dogs are public."

What I'm about to say might sound like a bit of a stretch, but if you have a special-needs child, you'll likely know exactly what I mean: Raising an average child is like having a cat—what happens in your home, stays in your home. Caring for a special-needs child, however, means you and that child are out there, making a fine old mess—right on the street—for everyone to see. People give you helpful hints, they scowl at your child's behavior—and they usually suspect that he is in some way rude or loud or obstinate or ill because you are. You know the saying, "There are no bad dogs, only bad owners"? I got a lot of "bad owner" looks when my son wailed, stomped, spun, ranted to himself, even licked people (he later explained that he liked how people's skin tasted salty in the summer; if only I could have invented a "porta-hole" for embarrassed parents to climb into during those early days with my son, I am confident it would be flying off the shelves at Target).

I remember once, when Toby was six years old, we visited a small beach town in Long Island, New York, where you had to ride your bike to get everywhere. A week with no cars, only tricycles and ten-speeds, was heaven. Until one day when a burly middle-aged man with a crocodile tan and a surfboard barreled down the bike path, heading straight for Toby. Anticipating what was about to happen, I sped up behind him, screaming, "Get to the right! Get to the right!" No dice. Toby panicked, skidded, tried to stop, then fell into the brush alongside the boardwalk. "NOT FAIR NOT FAIR NOT FAIR!" he hollered at the man's back as he sped off down the boardwalk. (Toby was a control freak at the time, and, despite knowing the rules of the road, he was annoyed that this man had not moved aside for him.) Physically, Toby was fine. I brushed him off, propped up his bike, and told him I'd walk it for a minute. Mentally, though, he was traumatized. He yelled and yelled and hurled rocks across the path as I stood calmly beside him and said, "We will sort things out as soon as you stop yelling." Just then, a woman in curlers stomped out from inside her cottage and said, "I know you are trying to teach him a lesson, but for goodness' sake, it's a Sunday! It's a holiday! Please take him away!" In my snarkiest voice, I said, "Yes, well, we try to save our tantrums for weekdays, but somehow my son must have gotten off his schedule." I wanted to suck the words back into my mouth, to apologize to her. But when I turned to say something, she'd already hurried inside.

At home, I had been safely employing the tactics our therapist seemed to repeat at every session: Let him cry it out. Hold him and tell him that you will speak to him when he is calm. But try explaining to the average Jane on the street, "Oh, you know, our therapist said to . . ." Some days, before we'd reined in Toby's behavior a bit, going out didn't seem worth the bother. But sitting home 24-7 wasn't exactly an option, either. Eventually, I found that the most effective way to manage expectations (and dirty looks) was to plan ahead and, when possible, to give people a heads-up. Telling friends we visited or made plans with about our quirks and systems seemed to make life less stressful for everyone. On a trip to Vermont with some family friends, for instance, I laid out the facts the first day: We won't be riding in your car. We're renting our own. Why? Because my son and windy roads don't mix. My friend got the idea pretty quickly after Toby lost his breakfast that morning on the way to go horseback riding. No arguments there.

Getting my point across hasn't always been so easy, though. After Toby refused to go swimming at day camp, I quietly investigated what might be bothering him. It wasn't the pool, Toby admitted to me. It was the noisy trip down four flights in an echoey stairwell, and then the frenzied chaos of forty kids changing into swimsuits that freaked him out. When I suggested to the staff that he arrive at camp each day in his swimsuit and that he go down to the pool ahead of the other kids, I got more than a few confused stares—but a kind counselor in training (CIT) offered to make Toby his charge.

The hair-raising arguments I've had with relatives prove one thing: It's often those you know best who are the least likely to change for you. I've occasionally had to let in-laws and cousins rail on me for my unconventional rules. After a while, though, I stopped caring what they thought—I'd made a promise to myself to be my kid's advocate, and I would rather shoulder their glares than give up on that vow.

The bottom line is that when people are unusual or quirky, it tends to make us uncomfortable. And nearly every page of this book is filled with moments in which a child or a family is primordially different. To successfully guide a child who has any disability, you need to (1) understand the differences between your child and the rest of the world, and (2) turn them into strengths as quickly as you can. This takes constant vigilance, watching and waiting for opportunities to swoop in and not only reassure a child with love, but teach her to succeed—quirks and all.

What can we learn from parents who are constantly faced with preparing others for the unexpected special needs of kids? In "You

Do Exist," Stephanie Dolgoff, thirty-nine, from New York City, the sibling of an autistic brother, drums up the courage to speak to a teenage girl she sees struggling to contain her embarrassment over how her autistic brother is behaving in the airport. Her piece shows that, with age, we gain perspective. Yet, it also points out that siblings of special-needs kids must become as skilled as parents at coping with the glares and looks and weirdness of having a not-so-normal brother or sister. Emily can now find the humor in Toby's odd behaviors, and she recognizes that people do not think of her as weird—even if her brother acts that way sometimes.

In "You Just Don't Understand," Rachel, a mom from Alabama whose child refuses to speak in public, writes: "I wish people would listen to me when I tell them about her mutism. I wish people would stop looking at me with those blank stares."

"Out There on Her Own," by a Massachusetts-based father, Dan, illuminates the lengths one parent must go to in order to explain his bipolar teenage daughter's disability to strangers. When she goes online to chat with men, and then arranges to meet these men in person, he calls the names and phone numbers he finds in his daughter's pockets and explains that she is a minor. What must these men be thinking when they get that call? The point is: It doesn't matter. As a parent, you are your child's protector, docent, translator, and representative, all rolled into one.

On reading these essays, I began to rethink how I have been introducing my child to the outside world. Could I do a better job of smoothing the way? I imagined the conversations I could have with teachers; I should have with friends; I may need to have with grandparents in the future. I've had many difficult conversations over the years—but after reading the insights of so many admirable parents, I now feel better prepared to handle life off the "normal kid" grid.

You Do Exist

Stephanie Dolgoff

Stephanie Dolgoff is the sister of a forty-four-year-old autistic man who lives in Maine, at a center for independent living. Stephanie lives in New York City.

L ast year, I was waiting to check in for a flight at Kennedy Airport with my husband and twin girls, who, at eighteen months, were age-appropriately licking our wheelie bag and hanging on the ribbon separating the twists of the line. As I prevented them from pulling the partition down altogether, a boy of thirteen or so next to us wandered over to me, took my two hands, and very sweetly kissed them. He then rested his head on my shoulder. I was surprised, but he was lovely, and it was a welcome respite from toddler chaos.

His mother immediately apologized, grabbed his hands, and led him back to their place in line. "My son Jeff is autistic," she explained matter-of-factly. "He is really into kissing people."

"Not to worry," I said. "My brother is autistic, too. Nothing to apologize for."

Then I caught a glimpse of his sister, who was roughly fifteen. She met my eye, then looked down at her Uggs, like she would rather be strip-searched by security than be identified as a member of a family that included a brother like that. I could practically hear her thoughts, because they were the same as mine at that age: *Oh. My. GOD. I am SO embarrassed! I know he can't help it but WHAT ABOUT ME? I mean, for once, could he just be NORMAL? I am going to DIE. Right now. And the worst part is, no one will notice.*

That much I could read on her face.

I do know that when I was a kid, whenever there was an incident with my older brother that provoked such treasonous thoughts—and there were too many to count—they were immediately followed by self-recrimination and guilt, to the tune of, *I am such a HORRIBLE person. How could I be ashamed of someone who can't help himself? He's a member of my family. I should be grateful that I don't have his problems and try to be more helpful. I know I should love him, but right now I HATE him. More proof that I'm a terrible person. I wish I could just vanish. Not that anyone would notice.*

B was five years older than I, and probably 150 pounds heavier—obese—with wild hair, dark brown, as we all have, and a booming voice. He was not into kissing people so much as talking to himself angrily, staring, shaking hands, and doing math calculations in the air with his finger. He also smelled putrid most of the time, despite the fact that he showered as many as three times a day. That may have had more to do with adolescence than his "brain injury," which is what people called his condition before the umbrella diagnosis of autism opened wide enough to include it, but it was no less embarrassing to me as a preteen and teenager.

We grew up in New York City, and my mother, who was smart and beautiful, with dark hair and brown eyes, advised me to cross the street when I saw someone muttering like a madman, because it certainly meant he was on crack or otherwise dangerous—except if he were my brother, in which case I was to love him unconditionally, not mind if his needs (dire though they often were) trumped mine, or if the family resources were disproportionately devoted to him. Most of all, I was not to complain or have any of my own problems, because Lord knows my parents couldn't handle one drop more. A teeny bit of this was explicit ("Christ, Steph, I'm sorry your friends didn't invite you to the party, but at least you have friends. Think about B," my grandmother famously said). But mostly it was implicit, or simply what I, as a child, divined was the best way to handle the situation.

The truth was, my parents were tapped, emotionally, financially, and in every other way you could think of. Their marriage was tanking, and my brother continued to require more of them than they could supply.

My response was to require less, much less, so that we added up to two normal kids. I was a straight-A-plus student, held two jobs outside of school, was involved in several after-school activities, and volunteered on weekends. It was a great way to never have to come home. By my sophomore year of high school, I also had a severe eating disorder and was as excellent at hiding it as I was at everything else. Occasionally my parents rallied the focus to ask me what was going on, but by then I knew to say, "Nothing much. Everything's fine." And they decided to believe me because they couldn't do much else.

When my brother was finally placed in a group home, and then in an independent living situation in Maine when I was seventeen, I felt liberated (then guilty for feeling that way), angry at him and my parents for how hard things had been (then guilty for feeling this way), and anxious to get away to college that fall, where no one knew me and I could start again (and, yes, I felt guilty for that, too).

It has taken much thinking and rethinking to untangle all of this, to realize what went wrong and to make peace with my parents and my brother over how things were handled. It's been helpful to remind myself that my parents were figuring it all out as they went along, that they had never had a child like me before (let alone one like B). Most important, I finally feel okay about being me—occasionally bitchy, uncharitable me—and that I am not a bad person for being human. I needn't be superhuman to make up for my brother's shortcomings.

So what would I want families with both a normally developing sibling and one with developmental problems to know? A family where one kid takes all the parents' energy, time, and attention? Exactly what I told Jeff's sister in the airport. When I had a second, I gestured her aside. I told her that I knew it was none of my business, but I understood what she was going through, and that it was okay to feel the way she did. That Jeff may take up more of the family's psychic space and that can suck, but that doesn't mean that she's any less for it. And I told her that things would get better and that she does exist, even if no one notices sometimes.

For an instant, she looked startled, then grateful, and then her veneer of teenage coolness hardened again. Still, I was glad I spoke to her. Even if I'm just some weird lady at the airport that she may never remember, I was pleased to be able to say to her what I wish someone had said to me back then.

Dream House

Scott Newport

Scott Newport is the father of Evan, who was diagnosed with Noonan's syndrome and hypertrophic cardiomyopathy as an infant. Evan spent the first 252 days of his life in the hospital, only to leave with a death sentence. Now four years old, Evan uses a ventilator to breathe and has various developmental delays. The Newport family lives in Royal Oak, Michigan.

Do you ever wonder how much you should explain to your children about a family secret? What if revealing that secret means having to sit down with one of your children and tell him that his sibling has a life-threatening condition? What will you dream up to say about his incurable illness? Should you tell your child that his sibling might die soon?

What a choice: to explain the whole, heartbreaking truth, or to just give bits and pieces when necessary. Not talking means saving your child from some of the day-to-day pain that you yourself, as a parent, are unable to escape. I mean, isn't that what we are supposed to do? Aren't we supposed to protect our children from the cruelty of life? Isn't that our duty?

Doctors are in the unfortunate position of having to share bad news all the time; the question for doctors is not *whether* to share, but *how* to share. Thankfully, our doctors chose their words carefully. It was July of 2002 when our son's doctors said the words that we'll never forget: "Scott and Penni, this news is going to be a great burden to you. Evan is terminal, and there is no cure for his disease."

Evan was born with a heart disease called hypertrophic cardio-myopathy. Fifty percent of children with his condition die before their second birthday, a statistic that is heartbreaking for any parent to hear. Six months after his birth, and while Evan was still in the pediatric intensive care unit at the University of Michigan children's hospital, Evan's doctors sat Penni and me down in a conference room just outside the ICU. The claustrophobic room overflowed with our family, some close friends, and the medical team we had come to know so well.

Again, the words float back to me: "Scott and Penni . . . Evan is terminal, and there is no cure for his disease." The attending doctor spoke to us with loving eyes; I am grateful for that.

The truth is, though, Penni and I already knew. Even though we're not doctors, we just knew. We'd already seen Evan close to death many times. And there were occasions when I thought to myself that heaven might be a good option. Some truths can't be hidden.

For me, the most painful words I think I'd ever heard came a few hours later, actually, from my wife. I had just returned from a visit to the hospital to see Evan. Penni and I sat alone in Evan's room (a mini-ICU we'd constructed in our home, for the day Evan finally left the hospital). Penni looked at me and said, "Scott, the doctor talked to me today and said we need to find a place to bury Evan." At that moment, I felt as though my very soul had crumbled.

Since then, I've had numerous opportunities to endure what life has thrown at me—we have a child with multiple disabilities, *an ICU in our home*, and a full staff of private duty nurses; it goes without saying that we're no strangers to the "tough stuff." Surprisingly, though, many of the most crushing words have come from children who don't understand the truth about a child who's dying.

One time I overheard my niece telling her older sister about Evan and his ventilator. She pointed to the ventilator—a machine about the size of a laptop computer, perched on a rolling stand and engulfed by hoses and wires—and said matter-of-factly to her sister, "That is to help Evan die."

Then there was the time our family went to the park, and a child who looked about eight years old yelled from the play structure that Evan and his older brother, Noah, were sitting on, "Hey, Dad, look, there's a zombie." I had to physically restrain Penni that day. I knew she wanted to start yelling at the kid, if not smack him across the face. (I did the mature thing and cursed him under my breath.) In my mind, I always thought a child might think the ventilator looked like a cool *Star Wars* gadget. And for some reason, I would have thought the kid in the park might have had a little humility and been thankful that he was able to move around the play structure so freely. I guess I was wrong. The experience made me begin to wonder how Noah really felt about his little brother.

Oftentimes, I've debated whether we've already told Noah, who is seven years old, too much about Evan and his condition. This past week, I struggled again as Penni relayed to me some things Noah said to her after another of Evan's life-threatening incidents here at home. What happened was this: Every night, Penni and Noah tuck Evan into bed. In the homey little ICU, Penni sits in the nurses' rocker holding Evan, and Noah sits on the floor. After Evan falls asleep, they lay him in his crib, hook him up to the ventilator and feeding pump, and make sure all the monitors are working correctly. Sometimes they'll even sing him a lullaby. One evening this week, as Evan fell off to sleep, Noah asked, "Mom, could I have another brother after Evan dies?" Noah, ever the big brother, loves to look out for Evan and help take care of him. And I'm sure that Noah—like all of us—will be crushed if that day comes.

Considering how much all of our lives have changed since Evan was born, Noah has handled things amazingly well. Even when he has had to miss out on fun activities because of Evan's limitations, he has simply accepted the news and moved on—which is remarkable, for a second-grader. This past week was the school's annual open house, where parents meet teachers and have the chance to see their children's classrooms and learn about what kids do on a typical day. At last year's open house, all of us—even Evan—showed up, but we weren't able to take part in all the activities because of Evan's medical needs. When we told Noah that we'd have to pass on the ice cream social because it was on the third floor and the line was a mile long, he was disappointed, but he didn't seem to mind. He's a good big brother like that.

So this year, Noah and I went to the open house alone. When it's just the two of us, he calls our outings "Dad Time." He was so proud to show me his classroom. "Come on," he yelled as he pulled me through the front door of the room. His neatly kept desk displayed a few art projects and short assignments that had earned him "happy faces" for a job well done.

Then his first-grade teacher asked, "Noah, did you show your dad your dream house posted out in the hall?"

"No," he replied, grabbing my hand and leading me off. I scanned the huge array of poster boards mounted to the concrete block wall in front of me. Noah stood next to me, silent and proud, allowing me to find his dream house myself. Each child's picture of a dream house told its own story. Each had its own dreamer. Bobby had a blue house, Sally had a house that looked like a castle, Rick's house was small, Gary needed a little help with color selection, and so on. Finally, I found Noah's, but instead of having just a single dreamer on it like the many others, it had "Noah and Evan's House" written on it.

Later that evening, Noah and I found ourselves in the school's old brick gymnasium. The gym, with its well-worn wooden floor, was packed with parents and kids eating ice cream. The smell of the gym brought back some of my own childhood memories, and as Noah played tag with his friends—weaving in and out of the fold-out tables and attendees—I thought back to the stuff I had seen on his desk. One thing stuck out in my mind. It was a crayon drawing that accompanied a school assignment called "Noah's News." The drawing depicted a little brother with a sick heart, coming home from the hospital for the first time.

The shouting kids soon brought me back to reality. All around me, parents were yelling at their kids for being too loud and for running too fast. But I didn't say a word to Noah as he ran past me; all I could think about was how proud I was of him.

When we got home, I told Penni about Noah's dream house. She replied, "You think that's something, wait till you hear what he told me last night." She said the conversation went something like this:

Mom, when Evan dies, can I put something special of mine in his casket to be buried with him?

It would be fine to do that.

A moment later, *Mom, can I have something of Evan's?*

Of course. What would you like?

Noah pointed to the ventilator, and Penni had to explain, *That's a machine we rent. It costs close to twenty thousand dollars, buddy. Daddy would have to work a lot to pay for that.*

But that's what I really want to have of Evan's, Noah insisted.

Curious, Penni had to ask, *Why do you want that, anyway?*

In his soft voice, Noah replied, *Because when I hear the ventilator giving Evan breaths, I know he is safe.*

The amazing thing about the whole story is that I love the sound of the ventilator, too. For me, each mechanical breath that starts with a swish of air and ends with a soft click reminds me of waves hitting the shore on a clear, peaceful evening, without a storm in sight.

So I guess you could say, all in all, I feel pretty good about what we have told Noah about his little brother.

I am sure that if we'd been less than honest with Noah about Evan's condition, he'd have probably figured it out, anyway. At least this way, he knows the truth, and the facts don't get turned around.

I know it sounds as though we have an unusual life, but I must say that it is a pretty amazing life, too, thanks to my wife and children. I'm too old to draw a picture of my dream house with crayons, but I like to think that mine would look similar to Noah's. I guess you could say we all have dreams for our perfect home. We dream that Evan will not die early in life. We dream that he'll live happily in Noah's crayon drawings, and in thoughts and images of him we'll always keep in our hearts.

You Just Don't Understand

Rachel

Rachel is the mother of four-year-old Karen,* who has been diagnosed with selective mutism. They live in Mobile, Alabama.

My four-year-old, Karen, is playing happily with her three-year-old sister, Ashley. She is chattering away about her favorite subject, Disney princesses. The sisters run around the house laughing and yelling happily to each other. To anyone looking in, it is a normal morning before school. Karen talks excitedly about what she wants to pack for lunch. As the time to leave gets closer, though, Karen begins to complain that her belly hurts. That she is tired. Anxiety about the day starts to build and excuses start; she has a thousand reasons why she shouldn't leave the house. Her shoes hurt. She doesn't want to eat what's been packed for lunch.

When I ask my daughters to get into the car, they climb inside, playing, forgetting where they are going and laughing. But when we pull up to our destination, Karen transforms. She becomes mute, literally unable to speak. The other kids are excited about the start of a school day, but Karen feels she is on display, center stage, completely scared of not knowing what to expect on this new day

As I help her out of the car, Karen is silent. She stares straight ahead, not making eye contact with her teacher, Miss Vicky. Ashley and I tell Karen we love her and to have a good day. She doesn't answer us,

---

*Names have been changed.

doesn't look back, and with her eyes looking at the ground, follows her teacher. Odd as it sounds, we are all used to this routine, because this isn't the first day of school, this isn't the first week of school—this is six months into her first school year, and the routine hasn't changed. I am not exaggerating when I say that my daughter spends her entire day at preschool—four whole hours—without a single word passing through her lips.

As a baby, I had noticed my daughter's sensitivity to noise, food texture, and light, and had her tested by an occupational therapist, who confirmed she had sensory integration problems. But it wasn't until age four, when we did some routine tests for school readiness, that a therapist told us that she thought my daughter suffered from selective mutism. When I got the diagnosis, I went home and immediately sat down at the computer to research the disorder. The descriptions of kids I found online fit with those of my own child: Karen had been an extremely anxious toddler, and she had severe stranger anxiety. As she grew older, her anxiousness took the form of mutism. One expert explained it this way: She is so overwhelmed by anxiety that her emotions literally "close up" her throat and make her unable to even whisper when she is not in the comfort of our home. She can nod on occasion, but mostly just tries to blend in with the wallpaper, hoping no one will notice her. She wears the same outfit every day—a green skirt, white shirt, pink socks, and pink shoes—so no one will comment on something new. She told me she tries not to drink anything during school since she can't ask to go to the bathroom.

As a mom of a selectively mute child, I feel I am on trial every single day. Grocery store bakers handing out cookies think I have raised a rude and ungrateful child when she won't even look up and acknowledge their outstretched hands. We've tried coaching Karen on how to respond with a thank-you—we even practice at home—but she can't make the transition from speaking at home to uttering even a single syllable in public. A few months after she was diagnosed, I even looked into homeschooling to end this stressful daily ordeal for her, but the research I found suggested that isolating a nonspeaking child is one of the worst things you can do for her. With homeschooling, she may never learn how to live in the social world.

So we venture out. Explaining the situation to other kids isn't easy, especially when they say hi to her on the playground, and she won't answer. I usually tell these kids that she just takes a while to get used to new things. In the safety of the car after a visit to the playground or a birthday party, she'll say, "I am shy, Mommy," or "Mommy, you know I don't talk to people."

It's painful to watch her suffer so much. I often find myself wondering, *How can I change the world, even just a little, for my daughter?* I wish people would listen to me when I tell them about her diagnosis. I wish they would quit insisting they are "magical with kids," and assume their special tricks will get her to talk to them. I watch as they pull out every trick in the book and keep talking to her, while she won't even look them in the face. I watch as they get annoyed or have their feelings hurt when they don't get a response from Karen.

When a child has a disability others can't see, outsiders are quick to blame the parents for bad behavior. I've heard them all: We can't control our children, we're too lenient, and we don't punish them enough. It makes me angry at the world sometimes. A little empathy would go a long way. I wish new friends, teachers, other moms, would stop looking at me with those blank stares when I talk about her diagnosis, as though I have made it up. I want to educate people so they can recognize this in their own sons and daughters, nieces and nephews, friends and neighbors; so they can help them to not feel ashamed. Let a shy child, or a selectively mute one like my daughter, come to them when they are ready. I want to shout, *Don't invade her space—pretend like she isn't there until she wants to be seen!*

Yes, I am angry with my daughter sometimes for not trying harder, but mostly I am miserable and anxious for her. I want to fix this and I can't.

And yet, the future is not so grim. Most children with selective mutism do eventually learn to talk in public. The process is slow and it takes years, expert research says. If people make a big deal out of their first words, kids with selective mutism will retreat further into their shell, so it is best to act like it is an everyday occurrence. Anti-anxiety medications in very small doses can help, and we are still working on one that will decrease Karen's behaviors instead of creating new nervous behaviors, like hair chewing and sleeve sucking. Since her disorder spills into other areas, like sensitivity to noise and textures, she won't try new food—too scary. She can't be left with babysitters or in gym or church nurseries—too anxiety-provoking. Friends offer to babysit, but I turn them down; Karen would be miserable the whole time, so I would be, too. We recently moved to my hometown of Mobile to be near my family. Thankfully, Karen is comfortable with her grandparents, which has allowed my husband and me to go out for the first time in years. It would be nice if we could find that special friend that she will talk to—just one, who is in her class, and who can be her voice. I could imagine that one friend telling the teacher that Karen has to go to the bathroom, helping her find a place to play on the playground. If that should happen, maybe Karen will begin to speak more. It may just start with a nod or a whisper, but I have faith that one day she will be shouting with confidence.

Out There on Her Own

Dan

Dan is the father of Jessica,* age seventeen, who has attention deficit hyperactivity disorder and bipolar disorder. They live in Massachusetts.

My daughter, Jessica, tends to be a very literal thinker. She is particularly poor at reading social cues, and her body language is often perceived as rude, inappropriate, and geeky. She often doesn't pick up on others' lack of interest in something she is talking about. What she finds funny, others often find irrelevant or even disgusting, especially when she uses foul language. She has very low self-esteem, and she will do almost anything—and I mean *anything*—to feel wanted. This can create some very scary circumstances. As far as our ability to protect her goes—well, I've learned a lot in the last few years about what, realistically, I can and can't do to protect her. She simply has no sense of danger or fear of strangers.

At seven years old, Jessica was diagnosed with ADD. As she got older, additional diagnoses, such as ODD and anxiety disorder, were added to the mix. At thirteen, she was diagnosed with bipolar disorder. (Her self-destructive behavior and lack of judgment are apparently typical of the disorder.) She sees a therapist once a week, and has for the better part of ten years.

As she entered her teens, Jessica's poor sense of judgment began to play a more threatening role in her life. Just after her fourteenth

*Names have been changed.

birthday, my wife and I found a piece of paper in her room with a man's name on it and an out-of-town phone number. I dialed the number and spoke with a woman who informed me that, yes, she had a twenty-six-year-old son living with her who did use the Internet to meet people. I could hear her turn to him and ask if he had ever spoken with or e-mailed my daughter. He acknowledged that he had (although I can't say for sure that he knew how old my daughter was) and said they had made plans to meet.

My heart rose up to my throat in anger. I informed the woman that my daughter was a minor and that I was immediately calling the local police; then I hung up. What my wife and I learned after filing a report with the Akron, Ohio, police department nearly killed me: Apparently, the man our daughter had contacted over the Internet had warrants out on him for beating his girlfriend and threatening her life. The police had gone to his home, only to learn that he had left after my call. Several days later they found the man, who had fled to relatives in Minnesota, and arrested him on charges unrelated to my daughter. We later learned that my daughter and this man met on MySpace.com. Since that time, the national press has exposed this site as making it too easy for predators to locate potential targets.

We were overwhelmed by our anger at this man and at our daughter. Why would Jessica expose herself to such a potentially harmful, if not deadly, situation? Along with the anger came frustration and disappointment in her poor decision making. Didn't we bring her up to never speak with strangers? I felt like I had failed in the role of protector of my family. I understood my daughter's issues, knew of the fearlessness that tends to be a trait of many bipolar kids, yet, somehow, I still was not able to help.

After this incident, my wife and I password-protected Jessica's computer, moved it from her bedroom to the living room, and told her she could use it for only ten minutes a day. Not surprisingly, though, Jessica's interest in the Web as a source of social interaction did not lessen, and she began to find any way she could to get on the Internet. Even with our vigilance, she managed to set up a new profile that included her first and last name, her high school, home address, and phone, and even a picture of herself. (Most likely, she set it up at an acquaintance's home, where there was no supervision.) I wouldn't have known any of this if I hadn't picked up the phone one school night to make a call and overheard her talking to an older-sounding man. I heard him say, "Just tell them that you're going over a friend's house to do homework, and I'll pick you up in five minutes." Our daughter replied, "I can't. My parents won't believe me." I immediately asked who it was, and he hung up. Our daughter reluctantly handed over the phone number of this person, and I called him back—then I called the local police. I wanted this guy arrested, too, but this time there were no grounds for doing so.

So for the past two years, we have monitored all of Jessica's phone calls when we are home with her. Nightly, we go through her pockets, coat, backpack, and handbag for any new contacts she might be making on the Internet at a friend's house, via telephone chat lines, or at the mall.

Luckily, our daughter, who is seventeen now, has not gotten into drugs, sex, running away, or staying out all night—we've been very fortunate in this respect. But we can never consider her to be out of the woods: Bipolar teens have a much higher rate of suicide—both attempted and successful—than other teens.

And my daughter keeps getting in trouble with the wrong men. Recently, it was a local adult-only chat line—an 800 number. She was calling in to meet guys. Each time we've caught her, my wife and I have asked ourselves (and our daughter's psychiatrist and our daughter's psychologist) when, when, *when* will she stop?

Unfortunately, no one knows when Jessica's behavior will change or improve—some therapists say the answer might be *never*. As I write this, she is on a huge cocktail of medication, prescribed by a great local psychiatrist and overseen by a brilliant psychopharmacol-ogist at Boston's Children's Hospital, so, for the small comfort it pro-vides, at least we know she's getting the optimal med types and combinations.

She is also part of a bipolar therapy group these days. The goal is to bolster her dangerously low self-esteem. I pray that it helps, be-cause our attempts at boosting her self-image at home have been mostly unsuccessful. Basically, she sees herself as a bad person who can do nothing right. She's also furious about our trying to protect her. At her age, most girls are experiencing some sense of freedom. Not Jessica. We screen every person she spends time with. She still does ungodly things in social settings, like announce to everyone within hearing range that a classmate "had better close her legs be-cause you can see things."

It is my hope that someday my daughter will read this and un-derstand that our motivation has been simply to keep her safe. But until she proves to us she really is capable of taking care of herself—and keeping herself safe—we will never stop our vigilance.

Friends Forever?

Ann Colin

Ann Colin is a freelance writer and former magazine editor. Her son Willie, diagnosed with ADD at age four, is now seventeen; her younger son, Nick, who also has ADD, is fifteen. She and her family live in New York City.

When your child is the "different" or "difficult" one, it changes your relationships—not always for the worse—although in the short term it might be.

My son Willie was diagnosed with attention deficit disorder (ADD) at age four, after a disastrous first year in preschool. Will's issues included not being able to sit still in circle time, not being able to share or use appropriate social skills in the block corner or on the jungle gym, and so on. He would either lash out physically at his classmates and teachers, or get so overwhelmed that he would hide under a table or in the coat closet and refuse to come out. In the months leading up to Will's diagnosis, my husband and I were shocked by how unintentionally cruel some of our friends were; it was an unkindness that manifested itself in the small things they said or, sometimes, in the larger things they did.

Because of his issues, Willie was the kid who was always in trouble at school, the boy who was forever acting up in public, the one on the receiving end of so many disapproving glances. It was bad enough when total strangers showed their disapproval—but even worse when it involved moms who I thought were my friends. I remember in particular one Saturday-morning phone call from the mother of one of Willie's classmates, Chloe, an ostentatious woman who spoiled her daughter, with whom I'd had coffee a few times after drop-off. "It's Chloe's birthday party today, and we didn't invite Willie," she told me. *Gee, thanks for sharing,* I thought. She continued, "However, I think we were wrong to exclude him, and I want to know if he'd like to come."

"Thanks for calling," I told her, working hard to keep my voice even, "but we have other plans." I may have also thanked her for being honest with me, I can't remember. I think she was under the impression that I'd already heard about the party, in which case, her phone call could be considered even more cringe inducing. Did she honestly think she could save face by inviting us at the last minute? Until she phoned and outed herself, I hadn't known a thing.

Talking openly about your quirky kid can sometimes bring out the worst in other people, prompting them to criticize you and your child—from the way you treat him to the way he behaves in school, compared to other kids. Even friends you know well or have known forever may start treating you differently once you have a "problem child," making snarky comments about your parenting skills or offering well-meaning advice that can wind up making you feel worse. True, there are some heroes who support you unconditionally, always showing up at the right time with a plate of chocolate chip cookies or a kind word, but angels like these are few and far between.

In my more generous moments, I remind myself that most—if not all—of these hurtful events were unintentional, bred from ignorance or, at the very best, bad manners. For example, one of my closest friends whom I have known since I was six was getting her teaching degree around the same time that Willie was being diagnosed. When we would meet for lunch, I would confide in her about the problems Willie was having—his trouble sitting still and transitioning to new activities at preschool, as well as developing social skills with his peers. My friend would nod attentively, but when I complained that his teacher seemed unwilling or unable to assist him in these areas, even though the school psychologist and the private psychologist we were working with had both come into the classroom to offer suggestions, my friend said tersely, "Well, you can't expect the teacher to give Willie so much individual attention. She has seventeen other kids in the class." I was stunned and wounded by her remark. Instead of identifying with my pain and concern for my son, my friend had sided with the teacher in knee-jerk solidarity.

It was a long time before I discussed Willie's problems with her again, even though she would often ask about him and the rest of my family. We managed to maintain our friendship by sticking to other subjects, such as her dating and then marrying a lovely man with whom she now has two children of her own. Life has a way of coming full circle, though—recently, while my friend and I were getting a manicure, she told me that her toddler was being assessed for a speech delay and would most likely need special-ed services. It was clear to me that she was anxious and upset about it. I took a deep breath before replying. I'll be honest: Part of me was thinking, *Well, now you know how I feel.* But instead, I dug deeper and considered what I would have wanted her to say to me so many years ago when the tables were turned. "I'm sorry to hear that," I told her honestly. "But I know you will get through it. You've got a terrific, intelligent kid, and everything else will be fine."

My friend never apologized to me about what she said—it was so long ago now that I doubt she even remembers the conversation. Maybe I should have spoken up at the time and told her that she really hurt my feelings. That would have given her the opportunity to apologize after the fact. The truth is, I now realize that I may have handled the situation badly, too. And who knows? Maybe the next time one of her friends comes to her for support in dealing with a special-needs child, she will know the exact, right thing to say—she will have found out for herself how having a special-needs child has changed her perspective.

SECTION 7

Seeing the Forest Through the Trees

Being in special-needs-parent mode for the past several years has transformed the way I look at life. And thinking back, I'm happy about that. I've developed a certain amount of moxie. Guiding Toby has given me the courage to write and to speak and to revel in being unaverage—and, if necessary, to blowtorch people out of my life who can't accept my family or me as we are. My prevailing motherhood theory these days is: I can pretty much tolerate any type of weirdness, as long as it isn't mean-spirited. And how wonderful it is to expand your concept of what's normal, particularly in your own home, and just run with what *is*. I am also more compassionate than ever. I think my son is a wonder, and some days I squeeze him so hard when I hug him that he backs off and says, *Mom, that hurts!* But I can't help it—I'm bursting with pride. Hokey as it may sound, there is a light at the end of the tunnel, instead of pitch darkness, when I look ahead.

Then there are those not-so-Hallmark-card moments. As I was working on this section, I heard a really loud crash downstairs. *What the . . . ?* I thought. My husband was feeding my son's gecko some crickets (Toby named the thing Geico) when the glass top to its cage fell off and shattered, sending shards everywhere. My son, exhausted, sad, and completely at a loss for what to do with himself, ran upstairs to my office and started yelling, "My lizard may not survive. Can we do yoga? Please? You said we couldn't, but I think we really should!" While we often do yoga at night to settle Toby down, I had told him no that evening because I had to work. It was already reading time, though, eight o'clock, so I decided to shut down the computer for the night, maybe even give in and do a Sun Salutation series or two on the rug, even though I was really in no mood. But the next thing I knew—in a strange mood reversal—Toby settled into an armchair reading an old Charlie Brown comic book from when I was a kid. "It's called 'Have It Your Way, Charlie Brown,'" my son told me, smiling, the irony not lost on him. When you have a special-needs kid, you can be confused, worried, and annoyed, all at the same time—and then seconds later, be fine with life. When you get to the point where you can embrace special needs in all its strangeness, you know you're in a good place. That is when you know you've seen the light.

It has taken me seven years to feel comfortable as a mom, but I am now as "obsessively committed," as one mother in this section says, to seeking out a "different kind of happiness for my family."

What might have been a long-term nightmare or insurmountable set of hurdles became a joy for the parents in this final section. And many times, I'm sure these parents thought this would never be possible. Celeste Soules, an Orlando, Florida, mom whose ten-year-old son, Ian, has autism, remembers revealing her son's disability to a group of moms with kids unlike her own. As she "outed" herself, she says she couldn't believe she was not being stared at, pitied, or judged. The group even shared a few laughs. Then there is Katy Parrish, a mother from Alaska, whose son is now an advocate for special-needs youth. Far from his hometown in Anchorage, he participates in a group called Kids As Self Advocates, which teaches teens about standing up for their special-needs rights. We tend to think of disabilities as something to mourn, but Celeste and Katy and many others in this book found the positive side of living with disability.

Often people ask me, How's your son doing now? He's a complete success story. Maybe that's why I compiled this book. Or, maybe, as my father suggested recently, an interest in opening new lines of communication for those with disabilities runs in the family—and *that's* why I undertook this book. My dad doesn't talk about his family much, but he made sure I knew this: In 1955, in the living room of the Park Avenue apartment where he grew up, my powerhouse grandmother helped a renowned psychotherapist named Jessica Horney found a clinic that still stands today on East Sixty-second Street in Manhattan, and provides psychoanalytic training as well as treatment. Horney was one of the first medical professionals to challenge Freud's theories about women, and her books compelled experts to take women's psychology and theories about women's mental health seriously. Some say she is a pioneer of self-help and self-analysis for women. Horney once said, "Concern should drive us into action, not into depression." She is also quoted as saying, "The perfect normal person is rare in our civilization." But my all-time favorite Horney line is: "Fortunately, analysis is not the only way to resolve inner conflicts. Life itself still remains a very effective therapist."

A little strange, I know, that at the end of this book I have decided to focus not on my own family, but on a psychoanalyst and feminist who few laypeople know. Partly, I wanted to do so because I am truly amazed at how far one courageous thinker—whether she lives in 1950 or 2007—can go to change the world. Just as Jessica Horney did, by speaking honestly, the mothers and fathers on these pages are changing the landscape of how we talk and think about special needs. Each one has seen life within the whirlwind, been brave enough to write about it, and is doing his or her best to replace heartbreak with hope. They know this: If you don't take advantage of life, it may take advantage of you. I hope this book helps you to see the light, too.

Dutch Boy

Anna Perera*

Anna Perera's son has been diagnosed with autism.

My son cried all night last night. Sometimes he does that. I long to help him, but I can't. He is autistic, they tell me, locked inside himself, inside a world that doctors tell me I have no access to. I don't know what he wants. He puts his hands on my face and cries, "Mamma, mamma"—one of the few words he can say—and I feel my heart break and shatter because I can't help him. It's like when water freezes and splits open a rock, there is no way to mend it, there is no way to stop it. My heart will always be scarred and broken by his tears.

When I first learned of his diagnosis, I was determined to pull him into my world. I sat endlessly trying to make him speak, make him look, make him do. And then slowly I began to realize that his world is beautiful, too. So I stopped trying to yank him into my world and instead tried to enter his.

We sit for hours at the fountain in town watching the water skip over the stones and cascade into the pool below. We fall asleep watching snowflakes drift lazily past the window, his cheek against

*A pseudonym.

mine, his hand holding my little finger. We watch a bug make its way up the wall.

I learn things about him. He loves the color blue. He likes Led Zeppelin and country music. He can't stand still when he hears the opening bars of a song he likes; he dances and giggles and gurgles until we all giggle, too.

He loves without restraint, without strings, without malice. His heart is so innocent and so pure. It is breathtaking.

He sees things no one else sees. To me it is a stone; to him it is a universe.

I read in a book once that having a child with special needs is like getting on an airplane for a trip. You think you are going to Venice, but then the stewardess tells you you have landed in Holland. Well, you can spend your time crying for the gondolas, or you can get out and enjoy the windmills. It's not quite what you had expected, but it is beautiful all the same.

So I call him my little Dutch boy. To remember that windmills are as beautiful as gondolas.

He fills my world with wonder and unbelievable joy.

Coming Out of the Dark

Celeste Soules

Celeste Soules is the mother of Ian, who is ten and has autism. They live in Orlando, Florida.

What's this? I thought, as I pulled a small white envelope out of my son Ian's bookbag one afternoon last spring. It had his name on the front, and when I opened it, an invitation to a roller-skating birthday party at a local skating rink was staring back at me. As I held it up, my thoughts turned to the other invitations we had received to attend parties and events for classmates of Ian's over the years. I always pictured a room full of noisy, active children having fun and playing together, while my son hid beneath a table with his hands over his ears. Out of fear and often out of embarrassment, we'd never gone to any of them. No parent wants their child to be on display, like a circus sideshow for spectators to gawk at and think, *What in the world is wrong with* that *child?* Not to mention, since people view the actions of your child as a direct reflection of you, you also have to battle the stigma that your parenting skills are terrible or nonexistent.

This time it was different, though. This time it was Jessica's party. Jessica is a wonderful little red-haired, green-eyed girl who had been in Ian's classes since kindergarten.

To understand how far we had come with Ian and his social skills over his first six years, and how his emerging social skills had even come about, I should explain Ian's school situation: During the first few years at his public school, my son split his time between a "regular" classroom and a "resource room"—a fancy name for a separate class consisting of an assortment of children with different challenges. More individual work, tailored to each child's needs, was done in the resource room, and small group activities (such as cutting, drawing, etcetera) were conducted. I believe that, for some children—those with very specific needs or a severe disability—the resource room is the best option. But I wondered if my highly functioning child would find enough role models to learn appropriate behavior by spending time in one of these rooms for a good portion of each day. Whether a child continues splitting his time as he gets older is a personal decision for each parent—if you have a good educational team at the school and a supportive principal (as was the case at Ian's school), you can gradually wean your child into a regular classroom.

When Ian was seven years old, I realized that, in order for him to learn how to socialize with children who have normal communication skills, he needed to be around typically developing peers more often. So, after many meetings with our empathetic education team, Ian gradually became part of the regular classroom, with the help of an aide. My argument to the school—the one that seemed to make the most impact in deciding to place him in a regular classroom full-time—was, *When Ian grows up and needs to buy groceries, will he go to the "special needs" grocery store? Or will he have to go to the store we all go to? When he wants to go to the movies, does he go to the "special needs" movie theater or the one we all go to? If we want these children to grow up and live and thrive in our community, they need to be in the community now!*

Once Ian was in the mainstream classroom full-time, most of the children genuinely grew to like him and were incredibly helpful during activities, when he would often have trouble understanding what he was being asked to do. Students would sit next to him and help prompt him along by showing visual examples and saying, "Like this Ian . . ." One girl, Jessica, really took a liking to him. I would find crayon drawings in his backpack every day, full of rainbows and hearts and a little rendition of a red-haired girl with a big smile, all signed by Jessica. In fact, Jessica's mom had been the first mother ever to ask if Jessica could come over and play with Ian at our house. She did come and play, for about twenty minutes one Saturday prior to the birthday invitation, and it went well. They basically just chased each other around the house playing tag, and then played video games together. An outsider would not have been able to discern who was "special" and who was "typical."

If the invitation had come from anyone else, I might have let my doubts and fears outweigh any desire I had for Ian to attend. But because it was from Jessica, I found myself having a hard time saying no.

The day of the party arrived, and we drove to Skate Reflections, in Kissimmee, Florida. Ian was oblivious to where we were going—but he was really happy we were going somewhere! (He loves to ride in the car and name the model of all the cars that go by. This is one of the odd autistic talents that surfaced in him.) As we drove, I was so nervous that my hands were sweating. I was thinking, *I hope he doesn't act too weird, I hope he doesn't cry, I hope the other parents don't stare with odd looks on their faces that read, "Oh, it is one of those children."* Pretty soon, I got myself so worked up that I started to cry. Thankfully, my husband, Arnaud, was extremely understanding, as always, and just kept repeating, "Honey, he has to learn about life with other children. You can't keep him at home forever!"

When we walked into the rink, it was a madhouse: loud music, strobe lights, kids screaming—the works. I looked at Ian, who was clinging to my husband and covering his ears.

This is a huge mistake, I thought. "We need to leave—now." But Arnaud insisted we give the party a shot. I was petrified: that Ian would have a meltdown, that I would be unable to control him, that Jessica would be disappointed if Ian, overwhelmed by the new situation, didn't act like the good friend he was at school.

We found the party sitting at tables decorated with balloons and gifts and a big birthday cake. I nervously walked up and introduced myself.

"Hi, everyone, I am Ian's mom." Jane, Jessica's mom, smiled and said, "Hi, Celeste, we are so glad you came! We were hoping you would be able to make it—how is he doing?" I looked over at Ian, who was still clinging to my husband and covering his ears.

"We probably need to give him a minute or two. Loud noises like this are tough for him."

Jane just smiled and said, "Okay."

A moment later, Jessica caught sight of Ian and ran over to him, yelling, "Ian, Ian, Ian!" When he didn't respond, she looked confused and hurt. I knelt down to Jessica and said, "Honey, the noise is hurting his ears right now. Let's give him a minute. He really wants to be your friend, you know!"

Arnaud told me to sit and meet all the mothers, then whisked Ian away to the rink's game room, while several of Ian's classmates and Jessica followed. Nervously, I installed myself in the middle of a group of parents at the table.

To my surprise, they were all incredibly nice! I think Jane had given them a hint of Ian's situation. They sat me down and started asking question after question—and more out of genuine concern, it seemed, than out of curiosity. They really seemed to care, they really were supportive, and they really made me feel like a "regular" mom. It was wonderful for me to explain Ian's disability, and, in fact, my disability—fear of socializing. After just a few minutes, I actually began to relax. I stopped shaking. I couldn't believe that I was actually being accepted. Think about it: acceptance. How many of us just want to be included? How many of us just want to be regular? Not stared at. Not pitied. Not made fun of. Not judged. I was so amazed—and grateful—that these other parents would take time to actually try to make me feel so comfortable. Many of them even shared odd things their so-called normal children did, and embarrassing moments they had in public. We all shared a laugh.

When I finally looked around to find Arnaud and Ian, what I saw stopped me in midwalk. There was my son, playing shuffleboard with Jessica. He was laughing, excited, smiling and jumping. He seemed oblivious to all the activity and noise. He was actually having fun—just like everyone else. Ten minutes later, he had a pair of roller skates on, with a classmate holding each hand, and they were trying to teach him how to skate. He was laughing so hard that all three of them fell on the floor in hysterics. Again, I felt the tears come—but this time they were tears of relief and happiness.

As we were getting ready to leave the party, every one of those kids hugged Ian and thanked him for coming. I felt like I had made some friends that day as well. Jessica and her family have remained close to Arnaud, Ian, and me, and we now make a regular habit of hanging out. Whenever we visit Jessica's house, Ian just walks right in and makes himself at home. Jessica treats Ian like a brother. And she actually taught him to swim underwater last year, after our numerous efforts failed. She just looked at him and said, "No, Ian, do it like this!" and showed him to hold his nose and duck underwater. It took him less than a minute to follow her cue. It is amazing how sometimes kids teach kids better than adults do.

Our newfound social confidence has also allowed Ian to meet new friends at school and in our neighborhood. And I have become friendly with our neighbors, too—instead of rushing into the house after work like I used to, always trying to hide Ian away, I now make time to chat. Today we take Ian shopping and to church—even to theme parks! And the more we take him out, the more we venture beyond our comfort zone, the more he relates to the world around him in a typical way. It's amazing how much one afternoon at a skating rink in Florida changed my life, and Ian's, too.

I wrote this essay because I understand. I know the panic, fear, and embarrassment we all feel, daily. I hope that our story inspires you to not throw out any party invitations you get, though, or hide in your house, feeling sorry for yourself or for your child. Give the world a try. It's waiting for you!

The Big Moment

Derrik Eichelberger

Derrik Eichelberger is the father of Jared, a thirteen-year-old boy with autism. They live in Santa Barbara, California.

All men dream, but not equally . . ."

That is the beginning of one of my favorite passages by T. E. Lawrence. I've held it close to my heart for years, but I never really understood how precious those words were until Jared, our son, graduated from sixth grade this past June.

My wife, Marcia, and I both looked forward to Jared's graduation with equal amounts of optimism and dread. He had spent seven years at Washington School, our local Santa Barbara elementary school. And it had truly taken a team effort to get us to this day—a team comprised of seven teachers, two principals, two special-ed teachers, twelve instructional assistants, one occupational therapist, five speech pathologists, one adapted physical education instructor, two determined parents, a school full of wonderful kids, and one child with a sideways grin and a gleam in his eye that somehow taught the bunch of them how to see the world his way.

When the big day came, Jared was struggling with a medication issue that had him out of sorts. After five years of taking a medication to help him with some of his behaviors, we discovered the medicine had suddenly brought on uncontrollable facial grimacing and blinking known as tardive dyskinesia. We hesitated letting him participate in the ceremony, fearing a disruptive episode. After much hand-wringing and encouragement from his aides and the Washington staff, however, we decided to proceed as planned.

As we feared, Jared was anxious. It was a beautiful spring day, and parents, friends, and guests were seated in a semicircle on the playground, facing a large stage with a magnificent view of the ocean and the Channel Islands in the distance. With ceremonial music playing in the background, Jared marched in with his friends and was then guided to us in the front row. After several restless minutes, we decided to move him over with the rest of the boys, hoping he would settle in. He couldn't sit still, though, so I decided to walk with him along the outer edges of the playground while young girls and boys read speeches and sang songs about friends and teachers and moving on. Finally, the big moment came, when it was time to file across stage alphabetically and be recognized by teachers and peers as a graduate. Marcia stood and turned on her video camera. I stood in the wings, with both of Jared's instructional assistants.

Though the school had rehearsed with Jared the day before, the routine had now fallen by the wayside: As Jared's name came near, he suddenly broke free of our little circle and ran full speed for the stage. I remember it now only in slow motion, a young woman receiving a handshake from the principal, Jared running full speed past her, and me trotting behind him onto the stage as fast as I could.

At the far edge of the stage, I managed to get ahold of Jared, and our little group—now including Marcia, who had run over from the audience—huddled together as quickly and discreetly as possible. We were shocked and embarrassed. Within a matter of moments, though, it was Jared's turn to receive his diploma. Perhaps in his mind he just needed to practice *just once more*. This time, without running, he walked up with his mother and an aide, and took his diploma graciously. And as he did, all the girls in his sixth-grade class rose to their feet and gave our son a standing ovation. The boys whistled and cheered. A rousing chorus of applause went up from all sides, kids and parents alike. We had tears in our eyes as our son looked out at his friends and admirers, basking for one brief moment in a wave of love and admiration. Tears flowed for thirty minutes afterward as friend after friend asked to have a picture taken with Jared.

Marcia and I have retold this story now many times to many friends. Each time, we try and explain just how hard Jared works every day, at his seventh-grade school and at home, struggling to communicate with just a handful of words, working for endless hours—with us, with tutors, and with peers—on what is so simple for the rest of us. While it's taken some persistence on our part, Jared is finally learning that he can't take candy from the store without paying for it, that he can't ride his bike on the yellow line down the middle of the street, and that for the ten-thousandth time, the tag goes in the back!

This is not the dream we had for him so many years ago: dreams of him throwing the winning pitch in the seventh game of the World Series, dreams of a fighter pilot disappearing into a vast blue sky, or even just the simple dream of a married son, handing us our grandchild for the very first time. Those are dreams for someone else now. But as we finish telling people the story of Jared's shining moment on graduation day, our pride swells in the knowledge that, despite all his challenges, Jared has become an ambassador for all people with disabilities, and that his spirit, humor, and grace have enriched the lives of everyone who has ever had the chance to know him. What parent ever dreamed a bigger dream?

Dwell in Possibility

Katy Parrish

Katy Parrish is the mother of fourteen-year-old Wilson, who has been diagnosed with hydrocephalus and experiences high-functioning autism. They live in Anchorage, Alaska.

On August 3, 1991, while cutting material for a maternity smock with a friend, I confided in her that I had just seen a boy in a wheelchair with cerebral palsy. I said: "I would never be strong enough to care for a child with special needs." That night, on my way home from her house, a drunk driver forced me off the road, and I ended up in preterm labor the next day. I was flown in a special jet from Fairbanks, Alaska, to Providence Hospital in Anchorage, where my son was delivered two days later at twenty-six weeks.

Somehow, during the emergency C-section, on the second cut to remove him, Wilson's umbilical cord was severed from the base of his stomach. He was bleeding from his tiny stomach, had no heartbeat, and wasn't breathing. Within twenty-four hours of his resuscitation, his head began to bleed internally. After 121 days in the NICU, two major surgeries, and a diagnosis of significant brain damage and hydrocephalus (caused when cerebral spinal fluid builds up in the head and causes an increase in pressure and damage to brain cells), Wilson was discharged weighing five pounds, four ounces.

Eleanor Roosevelt spoke the truth many years ago when she said, "The future belongs to those who believe in the beauty of their dreams." My son, Wilson, has taught me to dwell in possibility, not disability. In addition to being diagnosed with hydrocephalus, he experiences high-functioning autism. A week after his discharge, I took him to see his first pediatrician. The doctor—whom I'll call Dr. M— looked over his discharge summary, then asked me, "Have you checked him into custodial care?" "What's custodial care?" I asked.

He replied, "Your son will never be able to feed himself, walk, or talk, and will need twenty-four-hour nursing care."

I was floored. How did he know what my son would be capable of? I kept thinking, *What crystal ball is he looking into?* I didn't care how sick he appeared to be—that was not what I saw in my son's future.

I was furious at the way this doctor wrote Wilson off. My ex-husband was in the army at the time, and his insurance covered "well baby" checkups by Dr. M; I decided that day, however, that I would bring Wilson to Dr. M *only* for well checkups. For more involved medical care, I found Dr. Jeff Brand, in Anchorage—and I have never been happier with a decision in my life. Anytime I needed a referral for any kind of therapy for Wilson, Dr. Brand would write it the same day. Funnily, whenever I had to bring Wilson to see Dr. Brand, my son would pee on him—every time. After two years, this expert in the field of babies said to me with a grin, "You've done a wonderful job! I can't believe it! He's eating, walking, and talking! But there's one thing I just don't get: I've been working with babies for over twenty years and your son nails me every time." His validation of Wilson's excellent aim still makes me smile and giggle.

One of the most important lessons I learned from Dr. M was the value of a second opinion. Because I chose to seek help from a doctor who was optimistic, believed in early intervention, and trusted me when I was concerned, Wilson got the services he needed to make the progress Dr. M thought would never happen. Over time, it has become clear to me that the future is unwritten, and the power of the brain to compensate for damage is something no one can predict. Never be afraid to get a second opinion.

While Wilson was still in the NICU, his first occupational therapist told me, "You are the expert for Wilson. Believe it and live it." Her advice was a gift—she was so right. I took those words to heart and, since then, have read everything I could find on hydrocephalus, child development, sensory integration, autism, and the Individuals with Disabilities Education Act. I know that increasing my knowledge about Wilson's diagnoses and his rights to early intervention and educational services has made a huge difference for him.

My early successes with Wilson also convinced me to listen to my intuition when it came to how much and what type of therapy he needed. Seeking support from other parents, realizing that most of the answers will come from within, and carefully choosing my battles have also been vital in reducing the stresses associated with this journey. Wilson was seven years old when he asked me, while walking down the sidewalk, "Mom, why can't I ride a skateboard like Steven?" I explained, "Honey, your brain works differently than most people, and doctors call it autism." This conversation began the many hours of heart-to-hearts with Wilson about the damage to his brain and how he can overcome it. Being open with my child about his diagnosis, and giving him information when he asks, has helped Wilson transcend his special-needs label.

I've also noticed, over the years, that every mentor parent I have encountered has a unique sense of humor. Not only do I find comfort in laughing with them about things that most parents don't have a clue about, but I also find it keeps me sane, and empowers me not to give up when advocating for Wilson.

Some days are not so funny, of course. When Wilson was getting ready to transition from preschool into kindergarten, I remember the special-ed director asking me what I saw for Wilson when he was twenty-one. I replied, "I see him going to college or some vocational training program." She rolled her eyes at me. I realized then that it would be my responsibility to educate my son. Yes, he would go to school. But school was just one component of the overall education I envisioned for him—a broader education that involved people, and programs, and opportunities offered within our community. Given Wilson's amazing ability to see and remember details most people wouldn't notice, coupled with his generous and kind heart, I suspected that he might thrive in creative environments—and, as it turned out, I was right. Unfortunately, the public school systems in most American cities, including Anchorage, are more concerned with students passing exams than developing creativity and analytical thinking skills.

One of the most valuable community projects Wilson has been a part of is the Alaska Theater of Youth. This theater program runs a summer conservatory in Anchorage, where kids ages six to eighteen can learn more about acting, singing, theater technology, and video production. Most of the youth participating are, as Wilson would describe them, "neurotypical." He originally got involved in the program after I read an article in the autism magazine *The Advocate* describing the benefits of theater in helping children with autism develop social skills. Wilson loved the idea, and when I asked him which conservatory he would be most interested in, he chose the Technical Conservatory.

For the past three years, the program's technical and video staff has fully included Wilson in the conservatory, giving him true hands-on experience. Most notably, Wilson has helped create weekly "video news reports," which have been compiled into a promo piece to help gain funding for the program. The first year that Wilson was involved in the program, I was asked to hang around during rehearsals, in case he needed support with his technical and stage management responsibilities. After attending a few practices, standing backstage, he said to me, "Mom, do you see any other parents around here?" I acknowledged that I was the only mom. He said, "You can go get a cup of coffee and come back in a couple of hours." So I headed out the security door feeling proud that my teenage son had banished me from the theater.

Today, Wilson is fourteen and attending mainstream middle-school classes with some special-education support for math and language arts. He is teaching himself several languages, including Russian, Swedish, and Norwegian. He was the first autistic student to serve as the weather and sports anchor for the Mirror Lake Middle School Video News Team. And he has decided he wants to work in television news.

Last year, Wilson began participating in Kids As Self Advocates—a special project funded by the national family support program Family Voices—which teaches kids with disabilities about self-determination and advocacy. The project culminated in a huge conference held in Chicago—far away from our hometown of Anchorage, Alaska. The experience was unbelievably empowering for Wilson, who returned to Anchorage hell-bent on advocating for his right to ride the regular bus, after riding the "special" bus since preschool. After some initial resistance from his special-ed coordinator, Wilson reminded her he had a right to be in a less restrictive environment. Two days later, he was riding the regular bus.

This year, Wilson was chosen by Alaska's Governor's Council on Special Education and Disabilities to speak to our state's Senate Finance Committee to support new funding for disability services. (At the time of this writing, there is a huge waitlist in Alaska for disability services, such as job coaches, assisted living, and other invaluable resources.) Wilson ended his testimony requesting full funding for people who are "differently abled." Wilson's testimony, along with others that day, resulted in the first incremental funding to be allocated to removing people from the disability services waitlist in *nine years*.

From day one, I've told Wilson that he is the most wonderful and talented boy on the planet and that he can do anything he sets his mind to. Our nightly ritual before going to sleep these days is to name five things we are grateful for. Wilson always includes: "I am grateful that I can do anything I set my mind to."

Memo from the Department of Hindsight

Teresa S.

Teresa is the mother of Liam, who is thirty-two and
has severe learning disabilities, including hyperlexia.
They live in Illinois.*

My son, Liam, has hyperlexia, which means he has trouble with
abstract thinking. As a kid, he didn't follow directions well. He
still doesn't. (For example, if we say, "above the table," he might look
below the table.) Despite the fact that he could read the newspaper
quite well by age three, he had trouble telling a complete story. But
Liam could always memorize license plate numbers and birthdays—
he still does.

He is thirty-two years old now, and the days of never-ending
homework struggles and lonely years when he had few friends seem
far gone. But I remember being the parent of a young child, like
many of you probably are now, and asking myself: Can he—will
he—make it on his own as an adult? Here is your answer.

Liam graduated from high school in 1991 and has held a job as a
janitor for more than ten years. He gets good benefits on this job, including a pension. He has a nice group of friends and is happy with
his social life. He plays the piano quite well and enjoys it immensely,
as well as the accolades when he has the chance to perform. His
learning disability is still an issue in his life, but he is a responsible

---

*Names have been changed.

adult whom family members turn to whenever they need help, be it moving furniture, babysitting, gardening, or many other things.

Instinctively, when my husband passed away eighteen months ago, I knew life had to change—and this would be a big test for Liam. Again, I asked myself: Can he make it on his own? We had a big house, and until that point, it had worked out well for Liam to continue living with us. With my husband gone, however, the situation changed. To give Liam a boost of confidence in his ability to live independently, and to give me independence and allow me to move on with my own life, the decision was reached: I would encourage Liam to buy a place of his own.

My husband and I had often talked about this scenario, even before he became ill, and every once in a while we would ask Liam if he wanted to buy his own place. He would reply that he would like to someday, of course, just as his sisters had both bought places of their own. However, he would add, "Dad and you need me, though; isn't that right, Mom?" I would always confirm this and tell him how lucky we were to have him living with us and helping around the house.

After my husband passed away, Liam and I talked on and off for months about him finding a place, what that meant for him, and how we would handle it. One day he said, "You mean *sometime*, right?" I said, "No, Liam. I mean now. Is that okay?" He agreed that it was, but, of course, he is always so agreeable.

So we talked about it a lot more. That summer, after looking around a little, we found a condominium complex with units for sale, very near to the location Liam wanted: near his job and lots of stores and, even more important, favorite restaurants that stay open late, since he works evenings. The condos were in ten newly constructed buildings with twelve units in each, many complete and already sold out, others in some degree of completion and occupancy.

One day, we decided to visit the business office to see what the condos were like inside. The model on the first floor of one of the buildings was very nice, and Liam really liked it. Then we went to the model on the third floor. For some reason, Liam did not like this one. I insisted that he tell me his reasons for not liking it, given that it was brand new and the most reasonably priced of any we had found—not to mention the fact that it looked almost identical to the model on the first floor. It turned out that he did not like the way it was decorated. A very big turnoff was a picture hanging on a kitchen wall. I explained to him that the condo would be totally empty when he moved in, and he could put his own things into it. I needed to remind him of this again a few weeks later. He found this concept very hard to understand, but, eventually, he got it. And he decided to buy the condo.

Getting Liam to understand the financial side of the whole deal was difficult. (Considering his salary, he had a good deal of money saved, although I agreed to help him financially, to make his monthly payments more affordable.) We had regular vocabulary lessons. "What is a mortgage?" "What is escrow?" We had math lessons: "If you put this much down, how much will you still owe?" "If you only put ten percent down, how much would you owe?" Other days, I asked, "What will your lawyer do?" "What is the lady at the bank going to do for you?" Liam, who knew none of the answers initially, learned them all. I even encouraged him to practice signing his name quickly since he would need to do it so many times at the closing. I explained to him that his signature should not be spread out, the way he had written it in the past, and that penmanship did not count.

Looking back, I remember feeling uncomfortable when I thought people we met perceived me as an overbearing mother. But I needed to serve the role I did in the process. Trying to schedule an appointment to select carpet and fixtures with the sales representative at the building, a very nice lady about my age, she wondered out loud, "Couldn't he pick out his things himself? Do you really need to come?" I simply said, "Yes, I do." When I called the lawyer's office and arranged for him to attend the closing, I mentioned I would be there, and the attorney's secretary asked, "Why will you be there? Your name is not on the bill of sale, is it?" I said, "No, it isn't, but I will be there." Just before the closing, I debated whether to tell our lawyer that Liam has a learning disability. I visualized the lawyer whispering away to Liam about some problem that might come up at the proceeding, my straining to hear, and everyone thinking, "Poor Liam. What a dominating mother he has." So I decided to call him. I just said, "I want you to know that Liam has a learning disability just in case anything comes up during the closing. He might not understand everything you'll explain to him." The lawyer quipped, "That happens all the time. I say something to someone at the closing and the next day they call up and say, 'What were you talking about?'" It was as easy as that, and, remarkably, nothing did arise at the closing.

It has now been six months since my son bought a home of his own. Liam's confidence has gotten a new lift. As I expected, he is conscientious about paying his bills, he keeps his condo like a showplace, and he is a good neighbor. And at the same time, he is investing in his future.

I am always cutting the cord with Liam, little by little. Everything, or close to it, that Liam has ever learned has had to be taught to him, but with his success thus far in his role as homeowner, he has gained confidence in his own abilities and has become a happier, more self-assured man, proud of himself and his accomplishments. He is truly gaining independence, the ultimate goal of all parents. I wish the same for you.

Great Moments

Marie A. Sherrett

Marie Sherrett is the mother of Mark, who is twenty-five and has autism. They live in Upper Marlboro, Maryland.

One thing parents of kids with autism should know is the diagnosis is only a beginning. You have no idea how far your child will go in life. When told that my son Mark, then eight years old, had autism, I finally knew why he behaved as he did. What I did not know was what our lives would be like from that point on—how busy, exhausted, and challenged we would perpetually feel. I was not prepared for the heartbreak and disappointment I would experience time and time again, when babysitters or untrained teachers had no idea how to care for him.

As a guilty single parent, I continually tried to think of fun activities for Mark, but it was always hit or miss. He hated music classes and science programs. Malls were a nightmare. In movie theaters, he ran up and down the aisles. In parks, with his younger brother, Daniel, Mark ignored all of the other children, often appearing rude. In general, he just couldn't stand to be with strangers. So much for helping him develop social skills!

I tried to give Mark everything I could, but I also had to hold down a job (I worked as a legal secretary at the time) and raise my other son, too. Daniel somehow survived those early days fairly intact, despite Mark's temper tantrums, odd behaviors, disappearances, and our topsy-turvy lifestyle.

At time went by, we tried swimming and hiking and bowling to keep my son busy and focused. But the summer he turned nineteen, something I never could predicted caught his attention: therapeutic horseback riding. Through my son's high school in Annendale, Virginia, where the staff is trained to deal with autism, he'd ridden once or twice through a program called Flyingchanges. Flyingchanges encourages horseback riding as a form of therapy, stressing physical and emotional connections with the horse as a way to heal body, mind, and spirit. Initially, I didn't think I could afford to pay for Mark to ride more often—but then one day, I saw a photo of how happy he looked on a horse and was so taken with it that I called Flyingchanges, that I decided it was worth the sacrifice.

Mark soon began working with a wonderful trainer named Alex, who walked him through the careful training process needed to begin riding on a more regular basis. She taught him how to saddle, brush, feed, and lead a horse. Using reins was a new, intricate skill for Mark. In the barn, Mark walked a horse through elaborate mazes Alex created by placing poles on the ground and giving him verbal directions. Guiding a horse left and right prepared Mark for trail rides. On the days Mark rode, I was able to take short outings with Daniel or to go get a coffee by myself.

To me, when Mark was on a horse, he did not have autism. And the first time I saw Mark on a horse with my own eyes, I couldn't help crying. He stopped to ask, "Why are you crying?" and I told him I was happy. Here he was, high on a horse and tall in the saddle. It took my breath away. Memories of our years of struggles with autism raced through my mind, but here he had the situation under control.

I later learned that my tears had confused Mark. He could not understand why I was crying, but he knew something magical was going on. Back at home, he asked, "Is this part of my story?" I assured him that it was.

On learning about his new Sunday activity, Mark's speech therapist began incorporating horseback riding into their therapy. We would mail the papers Mark completed in these sessions to Alex, who proudly posted them for all to see. Throughout the next few months, not only did Mark become a more skilled rider, but his communication skills showed major improvements as well. After a year, he would even have conversations with horses he rode. Before his rides, he'd stroke the horse, lean his head against it, and speak inaudibly to it in a dreamlike state, bonding with it. Alex said this was typical for those with autism, and she would allow Mark time to do so. On bad days (like the day Mark "fired" me from being his mom!), I would fill Alex in upon arrival. She would then lead him on a longer route to clear his mind.

Jackson, a gentle brown horse, was Mark's favorite to ride, but he had one weakness: "I can't think why Jackson wants to eat poison ivy," Mark said to Alex and me one afternoon. Alex then charged Mark with the task of controlling Jackson's insatiable need to graze on the "delicacy"—and he did.

Now, at twenty-five, Mark rides at Piscataway Riding Stable in Clinton, Maryland. He wears a cowboy hat to ride on his new favorite horse, Macaroni. Mark trots there, rides through streams, and likes to count the deer he sees on trails. I've seen his self-esteem soar, and he's much better at taking direction. There's a calmness about him now, one that I had never seen in him before he began before riding. Our home is a showcase of blankets, towels, pillows, wall hangings, mats, books, and calendars covered in horses. Often, Mark puts his hand over mine on the car gearshift as we're driving home after horseback rides. "It's love," he says.

The Real Versus The Ideal

Todd Whelan

Todd Whelan is the father of Christopher, a three-year-old diagnosed with autism. They live in Lakewood, Colorado.

I am a single parent of a child who barely survived his birth. I remember the idealized dreams I had for Christopher before he was born, about how he would excel in sports, do well in school, achieve career success, and happiness in love—accomplish anything he wanted in life. On the day Christopher was born, in March 2003, I felt pure joy. He had survived, despite extremely high risks, including a torn placenta and being born six weeks prematurely. For him, survival alone was a miracle.

Before Christopher, I focused exclusively on work. I was a young attorney trying to establish myself as a solo practitioner and a community leader—to say I was materialistic and career driven would be an understatement. Then my son arrived, and my assumptions about life were turned upside down. After six weeks of waiting and wondering if Christopher would live or die, I was able to look within myself and recognize that there was more to life, specifically my life, than what I once thought.

I promised myself after this revelation that I'd be available to Christopher in ways my father never was for me. My relationship with my father was weak at best. He was a deeply introverted man, who never seemed to know how to relate to his own children. We had never shared the bonding moments I imagined most boys had with their fathers: fishing, going to ball games, talking about "guy" things. He never told me he loved me, never referred to me with terms of endearment, and was not there when I needed him to educate me about how to be a man. I never faulted my father for his shortcomings, but my thinking about becoming a father was dramatically impacted by my upbringing. Before Christopher was born, I wondered, *How can I be a good father to my son when I don't even know what it means to be a father?* Once I held my son in my arms, though, I made a commitment to be the most attentive and devoted father I could be.

My vow to myself was quickly challenged. By the time Christopher was six months old, I began to suspect he was struggling in ways that he could not express, and that I could not understand. I worried: *Would I withdraw as my father had? Would I find myself ignoring my son's struggles? What if distancing myself was the only way I could deal with his not eating properly, with his constant crying, with the way he ignored everyone in the room?* By the time he was three, Christopher's mother and I stopped taking him out in public. We couldn't handle his running off and throwing tantrums. Chris failed to understand danger—it wasn't unusual to find him running in front of cars or jumping precariously off slides at the park. And interacting with other kids would set him off, screaming or becoming violent.

Dreams of afternoons playing softball were dashed, for sure, but an even larger problem loomed: I realized I would need to reevaluate *my entire life* in order to give him the time and attention he was going to require. This would involve working part-time, committing to constant doctor and therapist appointments, and involving Chris in social activities, regardless of how he acted and the way it reflected on me as a parent.

It was around this time that Chris's mother withdrew and decided she could no longer be an active part of his life. Our marriage ended in August of 2005, and my role as father to Chris became intensified to a degree that I would have never thought I was capable of enduring. I was now a single father with primary custody of Christopher. I did not blame her for her feelings and for the route she took, however. I, too, often wondered if I could sustain a lifetime of challenges with my son.

This same year, Christopher was diagnosed with autism. The diagnosis forced me to accept that my son would likely face challenges his entire life. I did not abandon my hopes and dreams for him, but I knew how difficult each milestone would be for him to achieve. I continued tackling the huge challenges of having a special-needs kid—battles with insurance, finding appropriate doctors and sitters. In addition, Christopher was turned down at every day-care center we approached, which resulted in my providing his care twenty-four hours a day.

The daunting task of caring for Chris took a toll on my life in many ways. It's hard to admit this, but I began to question whether I even *liked* my son, despite my deep love for him. His constant screaming, physical violence, and inability to show any emotion made it very difficult. And the fact that Christopher did not reciprocate my love caused me a great deal of distress. I wondered if we would ever be connected emotionally—parent to son—or whether I would just be someone who cared for him on a daily basis. Could he ever see me as his parent? Could he ever show me love? These questions plagued me for months.

Then one day, not so long after his diagnosis, Chris walked up to me, threw his arms around me, and gave me a kiss on the cheek. I will never know what caused him to suddenly show his affection. I can only assume that, in his own way, Christopher was telling me that he appreciated everything I had done for him, and that he recognized me as someone significant in his life.

It was at that moment that I realized, yet again, how much pride and love I had for Christopher—and that I would provide him with something even better than the relationship I had so wanted with my own father: a sense of pride in every small stride he makes. Whether it's saying someone's name for the first time, expressing an interest in bikes and motorcycles, or simply being able to express his feelings to the point where he can climb into someone's lap and allow them to smother him with kisses, I will be there to give him the encouragement he needs.

Over the last several months, my son, now four, has made amazing progress: He has begun speaking more, saying "please" and "thank you." He engages other children in play and is more keenly aware of the world around him. I can only imagine that watching him learn and grow has turned out to be far more rewarding than anything I would have experienced if I had had an "average" son.

It's still hard, of course. And no doubt my capacity to love another human being has been tested by Christopher's struggles. I have laid awake many nights, thinking about every aspect of Christopher's life, and my own life, and speculated about how it all might have played out had my son not had autism. I have cried many times over Christopher's "lot in life," but I have come to find that I cry more often now out of joy for his achievements than out of sorrow. In less than five years, I have grown from a self-centered, materialistic individual into someone who would lay down in traffic for my son if necessary. I am also much more aware of the challenges other parents and children face, and I look at them with far less judgment than I did at one point in my life.

Nothing could possibly replace the joy I feel when I view with my own eyes how the care I've provided has helped Christopher develop. I know I have truly done something meaningful in my life every time Christopher surpasses another challenge, and that is the greatest achievement any parent can ask for.

Y.E.S.

Brenda Fletcher

Brenda is the mother of Brandon, who is twenty and has bipolar disorder. They live in Shelton, Nebraska.

In the last five years, Brandon has made more than twenty trips to Washington, D.C., and cities such as Atlanta, St. Louis, and San Juan, Puerto Rico, sharing his special-needs story. He is a huge success, serving on the National Youth Leadership Network for people with disabilities and as a member of a steering committee for a grant that will bring services to special-needs youth in our home state of Nebraska. But it wasn't always that way.

Brandon was such a difficult child that just before his second birthday, I began to question my ability to parent him. I remember asking myself, *Is God punishing me for something I've done wrong?* I was constantly asking our pediatrician's office whether there was something wrong with him, but it took until kindergarten for him to be diagnosed with ADHD and put on Ritalin. Even with the Ritalin, Brandon was constantly in motion and had difficulty sticking to a task or playing with classmates—I was fielding calls daily from his teachers, requesting help in controlling his behavior. I have two other children, and neither showed any of the same behavioral problems.

I desperately sought out doctors and therapists to help diagnose Brandon—and find a cure for whatever was wrong with him. By the time he was in elementary school, my son had more labels than a

Campbell's soup factory and had tried more than a few medications. None of this was easy on us emotionally. My family lives in a small town of less than fifteen hundred people. To say our community was less than supportive or understanding of Brandon would be an understatement. I had to endure lots of so-called friendly advice and criticism about my lack of parenting skills, whether it was teachers sending me newspaper articles or family members offering their unsolicited opinions. Members of the community also expressed concerns to the school board over how much money was being spent to educate Brandon. (I knew this because another parent mentioned it to me in the grocery store.) It was almost too much to take.

Although it was difficult for me to tolerate how my community treated me, it was nothing compared to what Brandon went through. As he grew older, it seemed like every day he was being taunted by his classmates and punished by teachers who didn't know how to deal with his challenging behavior. Some teachers turned a blind eye to the bullying at school, thinking that maybe a good hazing would "straighten him out." Many times he would come home angry and upset about his day at school, but he was unable to tell me why.

Then, in sixth grade, Brandon tried to kill himself.

Now, as depressing as this all sounds, let me remind you that this is not a story with an unhappy ending. After his suicide attempt, I transferred Brandon to a parochial school in a different town, twenty miles away. The idea was that Brandon would be able to start over. No one knew about his past behavior and challenges, and bullying was simply not tolerated at this school.

The new school turned out to be a wonderful place for Brandon. The children at the school were taught Christian values—values that were also extremely important to our family—and perhaps because of that, I think they were able to accept Brandon, despite his challenges. At this new school, my family was received with open arms, and instead of condemning my parenting skills, I was commended on raising such wonderful children. The change in Brandon was slow but steady.

After his suicide attempt, Brandon became involved in a program called Wraparound, a professional partner program for children with behavioral challenges. The program focuses on the positive—the child's and family's strengths—instead of on what is going wrong. When Brandon first became involved in the program, I was asked to choose a team of people who were important in his life, and who I believed would be instrumental in helping him. The group included formal supports, such as his doctor, psychiatrist, teachers, and therapist, as well as informal supports, like his grandfather, pastor, and friends of the family. I was treated as an equal by the entire team, including the professionals. Best of all, at our weekly meetings, members of the team listened to my concerns and suggestions, including my worries about how he would fare academically and socially.

Around this time, our family physician recommended that my son have a neuropsychological evaluation. The closest place to do it was in Omaha, a four-hour drive from home. After two days of testing, observations, and being seen by a developmental pediatrician, neurologist, speech pathologist, and psychologist, Brandon was diagnosed with pervasive developmental disorder. The doctors also felt Brandon had a mood disorder, and he was given proper medication. Working with a psychologist who specialized in children with autism spectrum disorders as well as speech, physical, and occupational therapists, we saw immediate progress. The combination of adjustments to his day-to-day life and therapy was life-changing. Brandon became more coordinated, a stronger reader, and better able to deal with his sensory issues.

For the first time in Brandon's life, he felt successful. He was not an angry little boy anymore; he was a young man whose challenging behaviors had all but disappeared. Still, I felt he needed to find out who he really was—to prove to himself that he could handle the outside world now. When he was fourteen years old, his Wraparound program director recommended he attend a Surgeon General's conference in Washington, D.C., addressing children's behavioral health. Brandon was one of eleven youths from across the country invited to attend.

At the conference, Brandon met other young people who had similar challenges. He heard stories like his own, stories of struggles with teachers, medications, misdiagnoses, and getting the proper help. He instantly connected with the other young people at the conference. But he and the other kids were upset by one thing: They were being all but ignored by many of the professionals invited to attend. He said it was clear to him and the other kids that none of the adults cared what they had to say, or bothered to ask them about their own experiences. And then an interesting thing happened: The kids decided to boycott that day's meeting, which got the attention of the Surgeon General. After some discussion, he allowed the kids twenty minutes on the platform to discuss their concerns—in front of six hundred of the top pediatricians, psychologists, and specialists in the country!

Brandon came home inspired and empowered. He wanted young people with similar challenges in Nebraska to experience what he had just gone through. He wanted others to feel accepted and understood. Brandon wanted to start a group for young people with behavioral health challenges. After being turned down by several groups, he approached Families CARE, a collection of parent support groups, and he and I spoke on a panel together about the issues of special-needs children. Gone were the days of being labeled a bad parent or a problem child. Now we were considered experts. I was hired to be the youth coordinator for Brandon's organization (called Y.E.S., Youth Encouraging Support). Brandon still likes to tell people "he got his mom her job."

My son had found his new obsession: helping others. His boundless energy and drive nearly exhausted me. I was (and still am) so proud of him; he had found his true calling and mission in life. He not only inspired me, but everyone around him. Others wanted to help out, and he found youth from around the state to join his group and cause. Y.E.S. spread like wildfire, throughout central Nebraska and beyond. And Brandon's efforts didn't go unnoticed. He soon began receiving awards for everything he was doing. He received a Freedom Award from our local newspaper, the *Kearney Hub*, and the Youth Medal of Excellence from the National Mental Health Association.

Brandon's Y.E.S. group started as a source of support, but it has developed into much more. The group is determined to show society that they are just like other kids with goals, dreams, and aspirations—that they are "normal." Over the past several years, they have been speaking out and advocating not only for themselves, but also for others with similar challenges who could not.

Shortly after Brandon was born, I often questioned why God had given me a child like my son. But now I realize why God gave me Brandon: He was a gift, a very precious gift, one who has taught not only me, but everyone he has known, lessons in life. Among those many lessons, he has taught us patience, tolerance, acceptance, equality, and perseverance to overcome obstacles to success. Most of all, he has taught us about unconditional love, and that there is light at the end of the tunnel for all those willing to find it.